IMAGES
of America

FILIPINOS IN THE EAST BAY

The Filipino American National Historical Society (FANHS) East Bay Chapter celebrates, from left to right, authors Vangie Buell (sitting), Lillian Galedo, Evelyn Luluquisen, and Ellie Hipol Luis for bringing to life the rich history of *Filipinos in the East Bay*. Their collaboration was a labor of love and an exhilarating experience as they inspired the community to portray their vibrant, multifaceted qualities. (Courtesy of David Bacon.)

ON THE COVER: The members of the first squadron of the Filipino Aviation Club were J. Tabarangao, E. Redable, F. Esteban (instructor), P. Esteban, A. Loyola, O. Valerio, and R. Miquel. (Courtesy of Esteban family.)

IMAGES
of America

FILIPINOS IN THE EAST BAY

Evangeline Canonizado Buell, Evelyn Luluquisen,
Lillian Galedo, Eleanor Hipol Luis, and
the Filipino American National Historical Society
East Bay Chapter

A

ARCADIA
PUBLISHING

Published by Arcadia Publishing
Charleston SC, Chicago IL, Portsmouth NH, San Francisco CA

Library of Congress Catalog Card Number: 2007943434

For all general information contact Arcadia Publishing at:
Telephone 843-853-2070
Fax 843-853-0044
E-mail sales@arcadiapublishing.com
For customer service and orders:
Toll-Free 1-888-313-2665

Visit us on the Internet at www.arcadiapublishing.com

This book is dedicated to the many people who shared photographs and stories for this publication and supported us in this project. We appreciate it and enjoyed working with you, and we take pride and are privileged in having learned more about our Filipino culture and history through your experiences. Because of space limitations, we were not able to include all the wonderful images submitted. All royalties earned from the publication of this book will go to the Filipino American National Historical Society East Bay Chapter for further documentation of the Filipino American experience in the Bay Area.

CONTENTS

Acknowledgments   6

Introduction   7

1.   Journey for Opportunity   11

2.   Expanding Community   31

3.   Changing Demographics   69

4.   The Journey Continues   115

Bibliography   127

ACKNOWLEDGMENTS

We would like to acknowledge all of the photograph contributors (their names are in the captions with each photograph), as well as family and friends who gave their unconditional support while we created this book, especially Abe Ignacio, Anita Ingram, Ben Love, Ben Luis, Bill Buell, Bill Wong, David Bacon, Dawn Mabalon, Dennis Ubungen, Eduardo Datangel, Mia Luluquisen, Isabel Luluquisen, Barbara Graham, James Moore, Janet Stickmon, Maria Lopez Tomelden, Geraldine Alcid, Mel Orpilla, Ron Muriera, Teresita Bautista, and Vincent Reyes.

The authors are deeply appreciative and grateful to the following individuals for their special assistance in making this book a success:

Cecilia Angel grew up in Oakland and was a navy WAVE. She enthusiastically assisted with contacts, gathering photographs and information. She was inspired and proclaimed, "I am acknowledging my being Filipino!"

Dennis Ubungen, counselor at City College of San Francisco, rescued his uncle Alex Hipol's photographs when he passed away. Dennis shared Uncle Alex's collection of Filipino community organizations, events, social occasions, and families. Dennis also shared the photograph that documents, thus far, the earliest account of Filipinos in the East Bay.

Lorraine Nicholas Rollins grew up in Berkeley. She kept her mother's treasured photographs of the buffalo soldiers and their families and still stays in contact with the early Filipino families of Berkeley. Her keen memory and storytelling skills provided the history that is scarcely documented.

Mildred "Millie" Lopez grew up in Berkeley. Her father, Marcelo Lopez, was a businessman and prominent Filipino community leader in the 1940s. Millie was instrumental in contacting widows, relatives, and descendants of community leaders, gathering information and scheduling interviews.

Rev. Michael Yoshii, pastor of Buena Vista United Methodist Church, provided work space for the authors to view, discuss, write, work on layout, and have our meals during lengthy work sessions. The work space allowed the authors to work effectively with photographs submitted for this book.

Vicki Garduno and her sisters, Lisa and Roberta, are the descendants of Felipe Esteban, who owned the Esteban Flying Service and was a prominent community leader in Oakland in the 1930s and 1940s. Vicki shared her collection, opened her home, and shared the photograph that is on the book cover.

INTRODUCTION

When the Filipino American National Historical Society of the East Bay got together to do oral histories in the 1990s, we learned that our people wanted to see their stories in writing. We knew that if we did not tell our stories in our own voices, then others would tell them for us. We would risk losing the essence and truth about the Filipino American experience. Our stories could fade from memory, and one day, our children's children would ask: Who are our ancestors? What were they like? What did they do? And we would not be there to answer their questions and, possibly, there would be nowhere to look.

We brought this book to life over an eight-month process of exploration, discovery, reconstruction, and synthesis. We talked with family and friends and networked with Filipino elders. For example, Vangie Buell reached out to Millie Lopez, and they reestablished contact after 40 years. It was through Millie that we were able to interview widowers and descendants of community leaders from the 1930s and 1940s. And through childhood family ties, Vangie contacted Lorraine Nicholas Rollins, who shared her mother's treasured collection of photographs, which document the migration of the wives of the buffalo soldiers in the early 1900s. Ellie Hipol Luis and Evelyn Luluquisen, born and raised in the East Bay, also drew on their resources of family and old friends. Lillian Galedo, a community leader in Oakland for over 25 years, contributed her knowledge and photographs of Filipino community organizing and advocacy work.

We collected hundreds of photographs from numerous family albums and organizations' archives. Contributors took the time to retrieve antique photographs and explore innumerable boxes long since forgotten. While viewing the photographs, contributors resurrected family stories they hoped to share with children, grandchildren, and great-grandchildren. For some families, it was the first time that prized photographs were shared with other family members. Many of our sessions with contributors became emotional as long-lost photographs were discovered and loved ones were remembered. We spent many hours listening to and recording family stories while scanning photographs. We realize that this book provides just a glimpse into our rich history and that the collection and documentation of the history of Filipinos in the East Bay must continue beyond the scope of this book.

As we scanned and reviewed hundreds of photographs, we recognized patterns and themes that brought forth the organization of the book chapters. We decided to incorporate as much historical context as possible within which these photographs captured the lives, activities, challenges, and achievements of Filipinos in the East Bay. We hope that as the stories in this book unfold through the photographs and captions, it will demonstrate to future generations of Filipino Americans that they come from a people who persevered through many hardships and lived life to the fullest. We want future Filipino American generations to take pride in their rich heritage.

CHAPTER ONE: JOURNEY FOR OPPORTUNITY

A brief description of the history of U.S.-Philippine relations is important to understand why and how Filipinos began immigrating to the East Bay.

At the end of the 19th century, the United States sought to absorb Spanish territories by attacking the Spanish in the Caribbean. Concurrently, a nationalist movement in the Philippines had just won independence from Spain in 1898. The Spanish-American War ended with the signing of the Treaty of Paris, ceding Cuba, Puerto Rico, and the Philippines to the United States for $20 million.

Filipinos valiantly resisted U.S. occupation, fighting a second war for independence from the United States, but Filipinos could not match U.S. firepower. Thus began the occupation of the Philippines by the United States from 1898 to 1946. The United States established military bases throughout the Philippines and a public school system based on English instruction, indoctrinating Filipinos with American culture.

During the U.S. occupation, Filipinos were considered "nationals" of the United States, allowing for open migration from the Philippines to the United States until the Tidings McDuffy Act in 1934 that restricted immigration to 50 per year. Those who migrated during the early 1900s were mainly students (*pensionados*), spouses of U.S. soldiers, and farm labor recruits. Filipino students were expected to return to the Philippines as teachers and administrators to further Americanize the Philippines. In the Bay Area, they attended the University of California, Berkeley; San Jose Teachers College; and San Francisco Teachers College. The Filipino women married to U.S. soldiers who fought in the Philippine-American War settled in Oakland, Berkeley, and San Francisco. These U.S. soldiers were mainly African Americans, known as buffalo soldiers. The Filipinos who were recruited to work as farm laborers for California's growing agricultural industry found jobs in the fertile Santa Clara and San Joaquin Valleys and in the East Bay's farms located on Alameda's Bay Farm Island, Alvarado, Centerville, Irvington, and Mission San Jose (now Union City and Fremont).

The first Filipino immigrants formed many groups to support each other in the racially charged climate that included Jim Crow laws, the Chinese Exclusion Act, and anti-miscegenation laws. As early as the 1920s and 1930s, fraternal and township organizations like the Legionarios Del Trabajo, Caballeros Damasalang, Bohol Circle, Tanay Club, Bauang Circle, and Cabugao Club were established. They took care of the sick, buried the dead with dignity, and provided small loans for crises or small businesses. Some also helped to organize unions to protect the rights of farm and cannery workers and participated in the union organizing drives of the time.

Those Filipinos who were fortunate to have homes, as opposed to living in boarding rooms, opened their homes to their *kababayan* (countrymen). The ratio of Filipino men to women in the early Filipino immigrant community was approximately 20 to 1. Filipino men married the few Filipino women in the area as well as Native American, Mexican, Puerto Rican, and African American women. Because of California's anti- miscegenation laws, Filipinos who married whites were forced to travel to states without marriage restrictions, then return to the East Bay. The early immigrants had no legal protections against the anti-Filipino laws and institutionalized discrimination that was openly practiced and socially accepted. Their *bayanihan* spirit (helping each other), strength of character, resilience, and dignity formed the foundation upon which the Filipino community now stands. The early families (Angel, Acebo, Canonizado, Lopez, Sacramento, San Juan, Esteban, Nicholas, Ymasa, Mendoza, Rivera, and Pulido to name a few) constituted the nucleus around which the community grew after World War II.

In 1941, Filipino immigrants joined the army and navy to help defend the United States and the Philippines against Japanese invasion. For Bernabe Saltivan, Eutiquio Bautista, Ambrose Loyola, and many others, it would be their first time in many years to return to their homeland. In the segregated U.S. Army, the Filipino 1st and 2nd Infantry Regiments were created. For their service, these soldiers earned American citizenship and veteran status. At the same time, 250,000 Filipinos in the Philippines were inducted into the U.S. military by President Roosevelt to help the U.S. war effort on the Pacific front. They were also promised citizenship and veteran status, but the Rescission Act of 1946 reneged on that promise. It was not until 1991 that eligibility for citizenship was reinstated, but that did not include veteran's status. As of 2007, legislation to restore veteran status is pending in Congress.

CHAPTER TWO: EXPANDING COMMUNITY

Many Filipino soldiers married while stationed in the Philippines or soon after World War II. The War Brides Act of 1945 allowed U.S. servicemen to bring their wives and children to the United States. This was a major contributing factor to the growth of the Filipino community in the post–World War II era. Filipinos also continued to immigrate to the United States as recruits in the U.S. Navy through the Military Bases Agreement of 1947, which remained in effect until 1992.

Oakland Chinatown was the hub of commerce and a gathering place for Filipinos in the East Bay. The "old-timer" contributors shared fond memories of the Elite Café, Manila Café, Baldo's Pool Parlor, the Philippine Cleaners, Franklin Electrical, George's Movieland Barbershop, and other businesses such as tailors and photography studios. They recalled that the single men could rent a cheap room, play the Chinese keno, visit a brothel, and find a good meal. Near Oakland Chinatown were Swans Department Store and Housewives Market where many Filipinos shopped. St. Mary's Church and School was one of the main parish communities for many Filipino families in Oakland. The Filipino community held events at Jenny Lind Hall, the Veterans Building, the Oakland Auditorium, and ISDES Hall in Alvarado. Filipinos maintained their connections with friends and family outside the East Bay and traveled to Suisun Valley, Livermore, Modesto, Stockton, Gilroy, Walnut Grove, Isleton, and Delano to be with loved ones.

As the post–World War II families set down roots, a vibrant Filipino community emerged. Many of the veterans returned to farm work, while others worked at the Oakland Naval Supply Center, Edy's Restaurant, and the Claremont Hotel. Women formed their own organizations, sponsored cultural events, and helped start family businesses. Families and friends celebrated many weddings, baptisms, and birthdays, and supported each other when a loved one passed away. Parents kept their children close and organized sports leagues, queen contests, and folk dance classes

During this period, Filipinos faced severe discrimination. Some contributors to this book recalled that whites viewed Filipinos as "filthy" and suited only for menial work and that their teachers steered them away from academics to domestic or trade classes. Moreover, Filipinos experienced few opportunities for advancement in their chosen field. Guillermo Valerio, for example, wanted to be a mathematician but only got as far as tutoring the University of California, Berkeley football team and had to make a living as a waiter and cook. Due to the Alien Land Laws, immigrants could not purchase and own their own homes. Non-Filipino spouses, sympathetic friends, and employers held deeds for Filipinos until the laws were revoked and the deed could be transferred.

Despite immense barriers, Filipinos continued to demonstrate their talents as writers, photographers, musicians, artists, and entrepreneurs. Augustine Lopez wrote a novel based on his life experience. Juan "Johnny" Lorenzo and Alex Hipol photographed many social gatherings that documented the lives of Filipinos in the East Bay. Joseph "Flip" Nunez and Ernie Tanuatco formed bands and combos and became renowned musicians.

CHAPTER THREE: CHANGING DEMOGRAPHICS

Major social forces and political events in the 1960s and 1970s fostered enormous growth in the Filipino community, nationally and in the East Bay. The largest wave of Filipino immigration was due mainly to changes in U.S. immigration policies and declining economic and political conditions in the Philippines. The Immigration Act of 1965 (Family Reunification Act), equalizing quotas from each country, made it possible to petition for immediate relatives using the family preference system. Difficult economic conditions in the Philippines and economic expansion in the United States increased immigration of Filipino professionals (teachers, nurses, doctors, accountants, and engineers) to the East Bay. Additionally, Pres. Ferdinand Marcos's 1972 declaration of martial law was the impetus for many to leave the Philippines.

The changing demographics are evident in many ways. Filipinos began participating in political and civic affairs, enrolling and graduating from colleges and universities in greater numbers, and gaining employment in many professions that historically barred Filipinos. Activism in the electoral process indicated the deepening roots and growing leadership of the Filipino community. Filipinos organized Browns for (Jerry) Brown in the late 1970s and Filipinos for Wilson Riles Jr., in the 1980s, and critically examined and organized against ballot initiatives (Propositions 187, 209, and 54). The East Bay was also the base for radical international political organizations like CAMD (Campaign Against the Marcos Dictatorship) and the *Katipunan ng mga Demokratikong Pilipino* (KDP). This international campaign was the most sustained and controversial political issue for the Filipino community from 1972 to 1986.

Building on the worker rights and farm worker organizing campaigns that began in the 1930s and the civil rights movement of the 1960s, Filipinos began establishing organizations that provided direct services and organized the community on social justice and economic and environmental issues. Filipinos for Affirmative Action, Filipino Civil Rights Advocates, and the Filipino American Coalition for Environmental Solidarity are a few examples.

Today in the East Bay there are over 10 Filipino elected members of city council and commissioners in city and county governments. Filipinos are represented in many professions, including chief of staff to elected officials, attorneys, judges, police officers, professors, marriage counselors, musicians, singers, dance instructors, and health care professionals. While the doors to opportunities for Filipinos continue to open, labor organizer Abba Ramos reminds us, "Most Filipino workers are still at the bottom. We make the beds. We work the restaurants, the electronics plants, and the fields. . . . we are a working class community."

In 2007, the Filipino population in the East Bay was roughly 100,000 and nearly 400,000 in the greater San Francisco Bay Area. Approximately 60,000 to 80,000 Filipinos immigrate to the United States annually. This influx of Filipino immigrants reinforces our cultural identity and languages. The combination of immigrants and U.S.-born Filipinos maintain cultural traditions that are essential to our community. Foremost are giving respect to and caring for elders, cherishing children, keeping family close, practicing spiritual and ritual ceremonies, getting a good education, maintaining family and social networks through gatherings that include lots of favorite homemade food, working hard, persevering, and supporting to each other during times of need.

CHAPTER FOUR: THE JOURNEY CONTINUES

Many of the Filipino immigrants whose photographs appear in this book began a journey of hope and adventure. Despite the vicious racial prejudice they experienced in American society, these early pioneers persisted in their belief that working hard, fighting for their rights, and honoring their own cultural heritage would build a vibrant Filipino community. There are now five generations of Filipinos in the East Bay.

Over the years, the community has changed. Filipinos in the Bay Area are less insular and actively participate in mainstream civic, cultural, and social life. Filipinos continue to branch out and marry non-Filipinos, building on its rich multicultural, multiethnic heritage. Young Filipinos are shaping a multicultural society, reaching out globally to protect the environment and are diligent in fighting injustices. They continue to create a society that honors basic human rights true to the principles of equality and justice for all. The book ends with photographs of youth fighting for social justice and expressing their strong Filipino identity.

One

JOURNEY FOR
OPPORTUNITY

The Filipino Aviators Club represents the pride, dignity, and adventurous spirit of Filipino migrants. Felipe Esteban (center) owned and operated the Esteban Flying Service from the 1930s to 1942. He was from Laog, Ilocos Norte, arrived in Seattle, Washington, in 1915, and then moved to Oakland with his white wife, Marie Keefir, in the 1920s. He later retired in Stockton, where he lived from 1948 to 1975. He was a leader in Kalapati Lodge 515, United Laoaguenos Association, Filipino Community of Alameda and Contra Cost County, and Grand Master of Legionarios Del Trabajo in Stockton. His granddaughter recalled that he was very good at taking tests. When he passed the examination for the U.S. Postal Service, he was told that he would be hired only after he agreed not to seek a promotion. (Courtesy of Esteban family.)

Maximo Tormes immigrated in 1904 and survived the 1906 earthquake. Julia Haya came as a maid to a *pensionado* whose wealthy family owned a sugar plantation in Negroes, Philippines. Not wanting to return to the Philippines when the *pensionado* completed his studies, Julia accepted an arranged marriage to Maximo. They were married in Oakland in 1918. The Tormes couple is shown here with their daughter Caroline around 1926. (Courtesy of Dennis Ubungen.)

Many of the men in this *c.* 1920s photograph came from San Fernando LaUnion, Illocos Norte, to work as farm laborers. Many traveled up and down California following the crops while others found jobs in the hotels, restaurants, and private homes of American families. A photograph of men only was typical of the time when very few single *Pinays* (Filipino women) were in the United States. (Courtesy of Dennis Ubungen.)

This photograph was taken during passage from the Philippines to the United States on the boat deck of the SS *Shidzuoka* on August 16, 1916. In the photograph is Augustine Lopez, who was to study in Seattle, Washington. Lopez eventually completed his degree in political science at the University of California, Berkeley and became a cofounder of the Filipino United Methodist Church in Oakland. (Courtesy of Mary Lopez.)

Marcellina "Siling" Nicholas is third from the left. Her mother owned and operated a bakery in Manila next door to a gathering place for buffalo soldiers. The women who married buffalo soldiers in the Philippines maintained lifelong friendships after they immigrated to the United States and settled in Oakland and Berkeley. From left to right are Mrs. Strickland, Bella Morrison, Marcellina Nicholas, Felicia Bunag Stokes, Mrs. Washington, and Mrs. Johnson. (Courtesy of Lorraine Nicholas Rollins.)

Westley Nicholas Sr., a buffalo soldier, served in Company I, 24th Infantry, in the Philippines insurrection during the Spanish-American War. Westley Nicholas Sr., charter member of Maj. John R. Lynch Camp No. 75, United Spanish War Veterans, worked at the U.S. Postal Service and settled his family in Berkeley. In this photograph is Nicholas with his wife, Marcellina, who is holding their eldest daughter, Lorraine, and Marcellina's sister, Felicidad. (Courtesy of Lorraine Nicholas Rollins.)

James McQuinney, a buffalo soldier, returned to the United States in the 1920s with his Filipino wife, Agapita, and settled in West Oakland. McQuinney willingly signed on a deed for Roberta Unabia, a family friend, when Filipinos were prohibited by law from buying property. McQuinney transferred the deed to Roberta Unabia when the law changed. (Courtesy of Lorraine Nicholas Rollins.)

Felicia Bunag Stokes Stevens Canonizado was the daughter of a buffalo soldier, Ernest Stokes of Chattanooga, Tennessee, who was stationed in the Philippines during the Spanish-American and the Philippine-American Wars. She immigrated in 1921 on the same boat as Marcelline Nicholas. Being half Filipina and half African American, she faced discrimination. She had a total of four children: Ernest, Russell, Evangeline, and Rosita. (Courtesy of Lorraine Nicholas Rollins.)

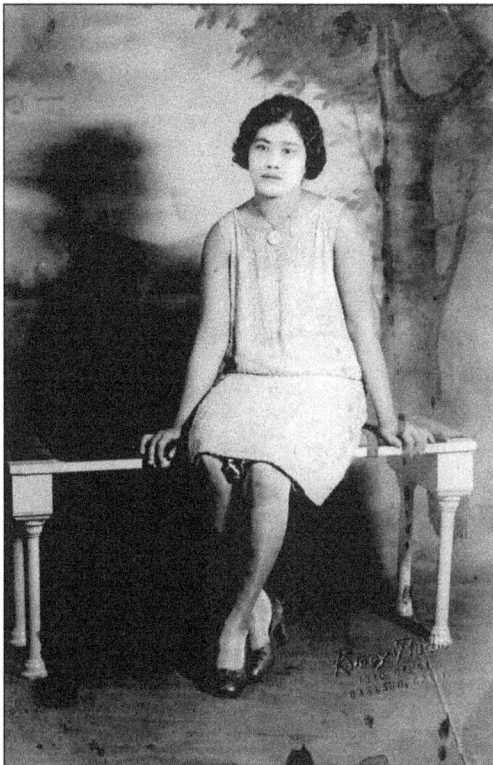

Roberta Dungca Stokes Unabia, born in Angeles, Pampanga, immigrated in 1928 with husband and buffalo soldier Ernest Stokes. Settling in Oakland, the couple socialized with former buffalo soldiers and their Filipino wives. Widowed in 1936, Roberta remarried in 1940. During World War II, she worked as a welder at the Richmond Shipyards while raising her deceased husband's granddaughters, Evangeline, Rosita, and Rosario. (Courtesy of Lorraine Nicholas Rollins.).

As a self-supporting student, Floyd Bongolan immigrated in 1928. He received a bachelor of arts degree from San Jose Teachers College and a master of arts from the University of California, Berkeley. He enlisted in the U.S. military and was sent to the Philippines during World War II. Upon his return to the United States, he worked at the U.S. Naval Supply Center in Oakland, where retired in 1987. (Courtesy of Mercedes Bongolan.)

Filipino men were known for their sharp appearance. Roos Brothers clothing store advertised in the *Filipino Students' Magazine* to the young *pensionados*: "A Los Estudiantes Filipinos—Si necesitais trages, sombreros, sobretodos, maletas de viage, etc., todos de la ultima moda y a precios razonables, vayanse a Roos Bros." From left to right are (seated) Eustaquio "Oliver" Valerio; (standing) unidentified, William Valerio, and unidentified. (Advertisement courtesy of Abe Ignacio; photograph courtesy of Joseph Valerio.)

From 1903 to 1910, the *pensionado* program provided government scholarships to students in return for government service. *Pensionados* were to represent the highest ideals of the Philippines as "Filipino student ambassadors." They attended such schools as the University of California, Berkeley; San Jose Teachers College; the University of Washington; and Massachusetts Institute of Technology. Filipinos who continued to study without sponsorship found it more difficult to stay in school. (Courtesy of Art Villaruz.)

Primo Villaruz Sr. was a man who had deep pride in his Filipino heritage and culture. After graduating from UC Berkeley in engineering in 1929, he was very fortunate to be hired as an engineer testing water quality for the State of California. With his earnings, he ran a boardinghouse providing food and shelter for many of his countrymen. (Courtesy of Art Villaruz.)

Filipinos worked as farm laborers in California's growing agriculture industry. As migrant workers, they followed the crops up and down the state. They developed friendships in their travels, building community networks along their way. Suisun Valley was a destination point for many Filipinos upon arrival. Few Filipino women were in California in the 1930s, as illustrated in this photograph of Lourdes Fernandez Lopez with farm laborers. (Courtesy of Mildred Lopez.)

This photograph gives evidence to early business organizing efforts by Filipinos in the East Bay. These delegates are attending the business session for the Third Inter-Filipino Community Conference from June 27 to 29, 1941, at Jenny Lind Hall in Oakland. On the stage are Felipe Esteban (third from left) and Augustine Lopez (far left). At the Oakland delegation table is Monico B. Luis Sr. To provide additional information about this conference, contact the Filipino American National Historical Society. (Courtesy of Paulino Love.)

These five young Filipino men became labor contractors. Ambrose Loyola (second from right) exhibited his leadership qualities at an early age by becoming one of the youngest farm labor contractors in the Bay Area. This photograph was taken in Concord, California, in 1929 or 1930. (Courtesy of Lulu Tipping.)

Estanislao "Stanley" Carpio Canonizado was born and raised in San Antonio, Zambales. He joined the U.S. Navy in 1917 in the Philippines. He experienced tremendous prejudice from white sailors who, believing Filipinos were monkeys, stripped him onboard the ship looking for his tail. He became chief bandmaster after Adm. Chester Nimitz heard him play his coronet and began orchestrating, transposing music for band instruments during World War II. (Courtesy of Evangeline Buell.)

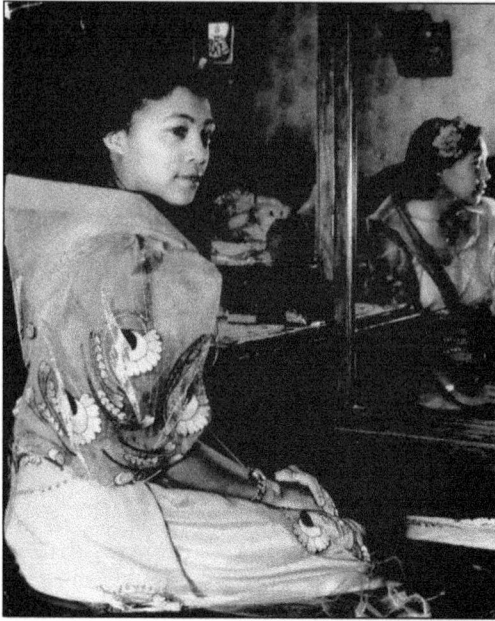

Marcellina "Siling" Nicholas studied piano at the Conservatory of Music in the Philippines. She was a pillar in the community, and many Filipinos sought her out when they arrived to the East Bay. She instilled Filipino values and culture in her children as much as she could. In these photographs, daughters Lorraine (left) and Ermelline (right) wore the dresses Siling brought from the Philippines. (Courtesy of Lorraine Nicholas Rollins.)

This photograph was taken during one of many Nicholas family outings at Bay Farm Island in Alameda with newfound friends and family. They are, from left to right, (kneeling) Raymond Acosta, Lorraine Nicholas, and Joey Pulido; (standing) Eugene Martin, Paul Ubungen, Emily Nicholas, Phyllis Pulido, Marcellina Nicholas, Abie ?, and Fernando Pulido. (Courtesy of Lorraine Nicholas Rollins.)

From left to right, the Asercion children, Arnie, Betty, and Andy, were born in California and moved to the Philippines in 1936 where their father's military salary would go much further. Living in Manila during World War II, they defended their home with a stash of ammunition. Upon returning to Berkeley, their parents became active members of the Filipino-American Organization of the East Bay and the Filipino-American Women's Organization of the East Bay. (Courtesy of Andy Asercion.)

Large gatherings are characteristic of Filipino culture. The young members of the Filipino Tennis Club included children of buffalo soldiers, young farm laborers, and students. (Courtesy of Lorraine Nicholas Rollins.)

The Junior Philippine Commonwealth celebrated their second anniversary in Oakland on November 14, 1937. (Courtesy of Dawn Mabalon.)

Legionarios Del Trabajo was one of the largest fraternal organizations to which Filipinos belonged. The lodges filled a social void and provided brotherhood. In 1925, the Kalapati Lodge No. 515 of Oakland was established and, along with the lodges in Berkeley and San Francisco, formed the nucleus of the Supreme Regional Council. In this photograph are the members in 1947. (Courtesy of Antonio Somera.)

Vincent Reyes Sr. arrived in Oakland in 1921 at age 14. He found work as a houseboy in Piedmont, where he attended high school and excelled in track and field. Between semesters, he worked for Japanese American farmers in Redlands, California. He was active in the Methodist Church and was an amateur boxer before moving to Los Angeles in search of employment during the Great Depression. (Courtesy of Vince Reyes Jr.)

The 1939 World's Fair on Treasure Island presented an exhibit of the Philippines, where Leonora Mendoza Rivera (Mangiben) reigned as Miss Philippines of the World's Fair. At the time, Leonora was approaching her 16th birthday. Leonora came to the United States in 1932 at the age of eight. She is the daughter of Maria Rivera, who owned the Philippine Cleaners in Oakland Chinatown. (Courtesy of Marie Yip.)

In 1936, the members of the Filipino United Methodist Church in Oakland were not allowed to worship in local Protestant churches. The congregation of 30–40 members met in homes and restaurants. Before settling at 1125 West Street, they were able to worship at the Congregational Chinese Church located in Oakland Chinatown. (Courtesy of Corazon Custodio Juralba.)

Rev. Raymond Fayloga, Juan Lorenzo, and Augustine Lopez were leaders of the Filipino United Methodist Church of Oakland. They had a major influence on the lives of the congregation's children, who were Filipino and mixed-race. Parents were encouraged to have programs that would include children. Represented here are children from the Casenares, Esteban, Pulido, Canonizado, and Catambay families. (Courtesy Evangeline Buell.)

24

Filipino navy men stationed at Yerba Buena (Goat Island) spent their weekend leave at the homes of Filipino families. For gatherings, furniture and rugs were cleared for dancing and an array of Filipino food was always served. Dance halls and public recreation halls were not open to Filipinos in the 1920s and 1930s; consequently, families would gather in homes all over the Bay Area. (Courtesy of Lorraine Nicholas Rollins.)

Francisco and Josepha Castaneda Alemania were from the Visayas and settled in Oakland in the 1930s. Leaders in the Filipino community, they hosted Cardinal Jaime Sin on his visit from the Philippines. Their children (Cesar, Armando, Francisco, and Lourdes) graduated from university. Josepha Alemania played classical guitar and was a member of the Filipino Women's Club of the East Bay. Francisco Alemania Sr. worked at Mare Island and Mills College. (Courtesy of Ellie Luis.)

Felipe Esteban lived with his wife, Marie Keefir, and daughter Patricia in Oakland. He owned three Porterville two-passenger airplanes and taught Filipinos to fly with his Esteban Flying Services from the 1930s to 1942. This is the only flying school known to be Filipino-owned. Esteban was also a licensed flight instructor and mechanic. While Felipe ran this business, Marie Keefir ran the boarding home where Filipinos could rent a room. (Courtesy of Esteban family.)

Members of the Filipino Aviation Club are pictured at San Francisco Bay Air Dome in Alameda on June 11, 1939. (Courtesy of Esteban family.)

At the outbreak of World War II, Filipinos who came to the United States prior to the war wanted to help defend the Philippines against Japanese invasion. In 1941, Filipinos asked that they be allowed to join the U.S. armed forces. The U.S. Army formed the 1st and 2nd Filipino Regiments. (Courtesy of Ellie Luis.)

OAKLAND TRIBUNE, TUESDAY, DECEMBER 9, 1941

TO BE PUT ON 24-HOUR

THE PHILIPPINES TODAY

Filipinos in U.S. Ask to Join Up

WASHINGTON, Dec. 9.—(/P)— Filipinos from throughout the United States are flooding the office of their resident commissioner here with telegrams asking how they might aid in the war against Japan.

A local group, led by Abdon Llorante of the commissioner's staff, a lieutenant in the United States Army in the last war, have requested Secretary of War Stimson to permit their joining United States forces or that they be given transportation to the islands where they may fight. They carried a letter from Commissioner J. M. Elizalde.

Filipinos are considered nationals of this country, but not citizens.

It had not been determined whether the joint efforts of the United States and the Philippine commonwealth against a common enemy would sufficiently alter the status of Filipinos in this country and Hawaii to permit their joining the military services of this country.

Hundreds of Filipino living in the United States and working as farm laborers, hotel workers, and domestics joined the U.S. military to defend the United States and the Philippines. Filipinos were assigned to segregated Filipino battalions and sent to the Philippines and Europe. In this photograph of the Anti-Tank Company, 1st Filipino Infantry, is longtime Oaklander Eutiquio Bautista. After the war, he sent for his wife, Flory, and child, Teresita. (Courtesy of Terry Bautista.)

Three of the 11 Saltivan brothers and cousins who came to the United States together in the 1920s joined the navy at the beginning of World War II. In this photograph, Bernabe "Benny" Saltivan (center) was in military service for 21 years until his retirement in 1962. He then returned to the East Bay with his wife, Aida Acevedo, and children, Benny Jr. and Eva, from San Juan, Puerto Rico, where he was stationed. (Courtesy of Eva Saltivan.)

Mariano Marzan served in New Guinea and the Philippines with other enlistees of the 1st and 2nd Filipino Regiments. His battalion served in infantry and saw many days of combat. After the war, Mariano returned to work and lived at Bay Farm Island in Alameda until 1955, when he went back to the Philippines to marry Soledad Mapanao. Mariano lived to celebrate his 100th birthday in 2004. (Courtesy of Jimmy Marzan.)

Ambrocio Angel immigrated at age 16 in the 1930s. He left the University of California, Berkeley when a professor unfairly lowered his grade in disbelief of high test results. Strong in character and fortitude and highly respected, he completed a distinguished 30-year career in the U.S. Coast Guard, raised five children, built two houses in Oakland, and owned the Galley restaurant with his wife, Marina. (Courtesy of Cecilia Angel.)

AMBROSIO Q. ANGEL AND MARIAM ANGEL

OUR MOTHER IN THE 1940'S

FIVE CENTS

F 00334734 F

1942 —MILITARY PAYMENT CERTIFICATE FOR MILITARY BASE USE ONLY. 5 CENTS.

WELDER IN 1943

THREE POSITIONS
FLAT-VERTICAL AND OVERHEAD
EMPLOYED SHIPBUILDING DIVISION
OF PERMANENTE METALS CORPORATION,
KAISER COMPANY, INC.

Marina Angel worked as a welder in the Richmond Shipyard with other women during World War II. They were compensated with a salary and given coupons that could be redeemed on base for food. Due to some Filipino women's petite physical size, they were chosen to crawl into the confined spaces of ships to weld. Marina's father was a U.S. soldier stationed in the Philippines in the early 1900s. (Courtesy of Cecilia Angel.)

Many army men got married in the Philippines before the end of their military term. Newlyweds Daniel and Dominica Tabisaura are shown around 1945. While Daniel completed his tour in the Philippines, Dominica came to the United States on her own in 1948 with their oldest daughter, Helen. She was joined a year later in the United States by her husband. (Courtesy of Christine Tabisaura.)

Mateo and Ponciana Caranay were wed in the Philippines before Mateo's military term ended. Ponciana came to the United States with their daughter Caroline in 1948 with the help of the Red Cross. Ponciana did not want to leave her own family and familiar surroundings in the Philippines. She felt she had no choice but to follow her husband to the United States. The Caranay family settled in Alameda. (Courtesy of Ponciana Caranay.)

Two

EXPANDING COMMUNITY

The War Brides Act of 1946 allowed World War II servicemen to bring their wives and naturalized children to the United States. Several of the women in this 1952 photograph are war brides who met in Samar, Philippines, where they stayed with their husbands before the military shipped the servicemen back to the United States. These war brides then went back to their hometowns to wait for their paperwork that would allow them to come to the United States. Some of the women made their first homes in farm worker housing on Bay Farm Island, where their husbands were employed. Some lived in other parts of the East Bay. A close bond, which exists to this day, formed between them to ease their homesickness for family and friends they left behind. Included in this photograph are, from left to right, Dominica Tabisaura, Constancia Pastrana, Bibang ?, Engracia Hipol, Trinidad Saltivan, Ponciana Caranay, and Concepcion Mina. (Courtesy of Ponciana Caranay.)

Filipino women—*Pinays*—are the backbone of the Filipino community. In this the post–World War II photograph, military wives and other women in the Filipino community gathered. These women would eventually form their own organizations to maintain cultural traditions and strengthen community ties. Shown are, from left to right, (seated) Sexta Vinluan, Juanita San Juan, Doris Fernandez, and Mary Lopez; (standing) Anita Rosario, Julia Fernandez, Carmen Valerio, unidentified, Lourdes Lopez, Carmen Mapanao, and four unidentified. (Courtesy of Carmen Mapanao.)

The Philippine Christmas Parol, "A Bamboo Star of Hope," (a bamboo sculpture and decorated star) shined brightly on Adeline Street during World War II. Estanislao Canonizado reunited with his family in 1946. From left to right are Manuel Unabia, Roberta Unabia, Evangeline Canonizado (Buell), Rosario Unabia (Garcia), Stanley Canonizado, and Rosita Canonizado (Dietrich). (Courtesy of Vangie Buell.)

After World War II, Honorio Hipol returned to the United States and processed paperwork for his fiancée, Engracia Pada-on, to join him. Engracia came to the United States in 1947, and they were married at St. Mary's Church in West Oakland. This 1948 photograph was taken in downtown Oakland (in the background is the Tribune building tower), where the Filipino community socialized at many of the Filipino-owned businesses. (Photograph by Alex Hipol.)

In 1943, Mary Dickson planned to study Chinese before going to China to work as a missionary. Instead she was sent to the Filipino United Methodist Church in Oakland to teach Sunday school. There she met Augustine Lopez, who was a minister in the church. In 1946, the couple traveled to Seattle, Washington, where it was legal for a Filipino man to marry a white woman. (Courtesy of Mary Lopez.)

War brides Flory (left) and Maura (center) joined their husbands Eutiquio Bautista and Saturnino Dulay Laigo to live in Oakland after World War II. Pictured here are toddlers Terry Bautista (center) and Avelino Laigo (left). (The other woman in this photograph is unidentified.) (Courtesy of Teresita Bautista.)

This 1951 photograph shows the baby boom of the 1950s. The number of war brides increased, and friendships blossomed among them. Their bond was based on many commonalities, such as townships, relatives, the war, World War II military husbands, travel stories, and growing families. (Courtesy of Engracia Hipol.)

In the 1950s, migrant farm workers in Irvington (now part of the city of Fremont) lived in housing provided on the Bailey farm, where Mission San Jose High School is located today. A number of Filipino families, including the Rabello, Jesuitas, Cabarar, and Ugale families, lived and worked on this farm. This photograph commemorates Boyd Rabello's christening celebration. (Courtesy of Rosita Valerio.)

The Filipino Ladies Association of the East Bay was a large organization whose members were mostly the war brides from Berkeley and cities close by. They hosted gala social events where the attendees dressed in traditional Filipino formal wear—the terno dress and barong Tagalog shirts. (Courtesy of Carmen Mapanao.)

Children are dear to the Filipino family. The Filipino culture is passed on through the family's active participation in community events. These little girls are modeling the Filipino terno, a traditional dress with "butterfly" sleeves. (Courtesy of Carmen Mapanao.)

The Tanay Club of America, established in 1924, was one of the largest town organizations in the East Bay. From left to right, the Mendoza sisters—Orpha, Remedios, Arceli, and Mercedes—and Mercedes's daughter, Meriann, were active members of the organization. The organization is still active today with an office in Oakland. (Courtesy of Arlene Picar.)

These *Dalagas* (young single Filipino women) were members of the Mabuhay Club at St. Mary's Immaculate Conception Church in Oakland in 1947. From left to right are (seated on the floor) Ray Aguila; (standing) Lucy Catambay (Bubenheim), Anita Aguila (Acebo), Margaret Acebo (Davis), Susan Reyes (Santamaria), Emily Ymasa (Guild), Mary del Rosario, Frances Caventa, Leticia Perez (del Rosario), Georgia Sacramento (Lenida), Frances Dela Rosa, Lorraine Francis, and Lilia Acebo. (Courtesy of Terry Acebo Davis.)

Celebrations at the Santos family home always included a houseful of guests. In this photograph, the Santos and Guzman family exchange gifts on Christmas day. (Courtesy of Linda Haraguchi.)

These Filipino students of the "bridge generation," who were born in the 1930s and 1940s, are in attendance at a gathering at Newman Hall near the University of California, Berkeley. Included in this photograph are members of the Mendoza family: Elizabeth, Benjamin, Patricia, and Albert. (Courtesy of Elizabeth Mendoza Megino.)

Teenagers gathered before a UC Berkeley football game in the 1950s. They are, from left to right, (first row) Maggie Acebo, Susie de los Reyes, Mildred Lopez, Georgia Sacramento, unidentified, and Sophie Ymasa (with eyes closed); (second row) unidentified, Rey Acebo, Ernie Bautista, unidentified, Fred Casineras, Lorraine Francisco, Florence Fernandez, Dolores Escalante, Clarita San Juan, Bro Moga, Emily Ymasa, and ? Escalante; (third row) Leo Escalante, unidentified, Arsenio Ascercion, Agrapino Cerbatos, and unidentified. (Courtesy of Mildred Lopez.)

Maura Ymasa was sponsored as a student by the Rich family of Berkeley. She married Sylvano Ymasa, and they had two daughters, Emily and Sophie. From left to right are Emily, Juan "Johnny" Lorenzo, and Sophie. Lorenzo was a photographer and was active in the Filipino United Methodist Church. He completed his bachelor of arts and retired from Oakland Army Supply Center. His beautiful penmanship adorned hundreds of diplomas. (Courtesy of Corazon Juralba.)

A funeral for a Filipino is a celebration of life, giving full respect to the person who has passed on. The top photograph shows the gathering at the funeral home for the final viewing on the night before the burial for a member of the Binmaley, Caloocan township organization. The bottom photograph depicts the honor, respect, and dignity paid to the deceased, which includes military pallbearers and the formal dress of the attendees. After the burial, those who attend the funeral service gather together for a meal. This is also a time to reunite with old friends and family. (Courtesy of Linda Guzman Haraguchi.)

American Legion Rizal Post 598 celebrated Father's Day with a picnic at the Hayward Plunge in the 1950s. Meat was cooked on the barbeque pit, and families brought food for all to share. Parents and their children enjoyed swimming, tennis, hiking, and relay games. The highlight of the day was a tug-of-war between the men and the boys. (Courtesy of Dennis Ubungen.)

Leonila Guzman came to the United States in 1949 and quickly acclimated to the lifestyle. Here she sits on the motorcycle with Dick Aquino. She was a very active member of the Filipino community, with membership in many civic and township organizations, such as the Filipino Women's Club of the East Bay. (Courtesy of Linda Haraguchi.)

41

The American Legion Rizal Post 598 was established after World War II and named in honor of the illustrious Jose Rizal of the Philippines. Veterans who served in various armed forces units during the war were encouraged to join this Oakland-based organization. The auxiliary unit composed of wives of the post was later established. (Courtesy of Engracia Hipol.)

Alex Hipol could be found at just about every event with his camera constantly flashing. A photographer who worked outside of a studio, he captured the Filipino (and non-Filipino) community from the late 1920s to the 1990s. He was also an artist who worked with oil and ink media. This is an oil portrait of Rebecca Austria, a concert pianist and piano teacher. (Courtesy of Dennis Ubungen.)

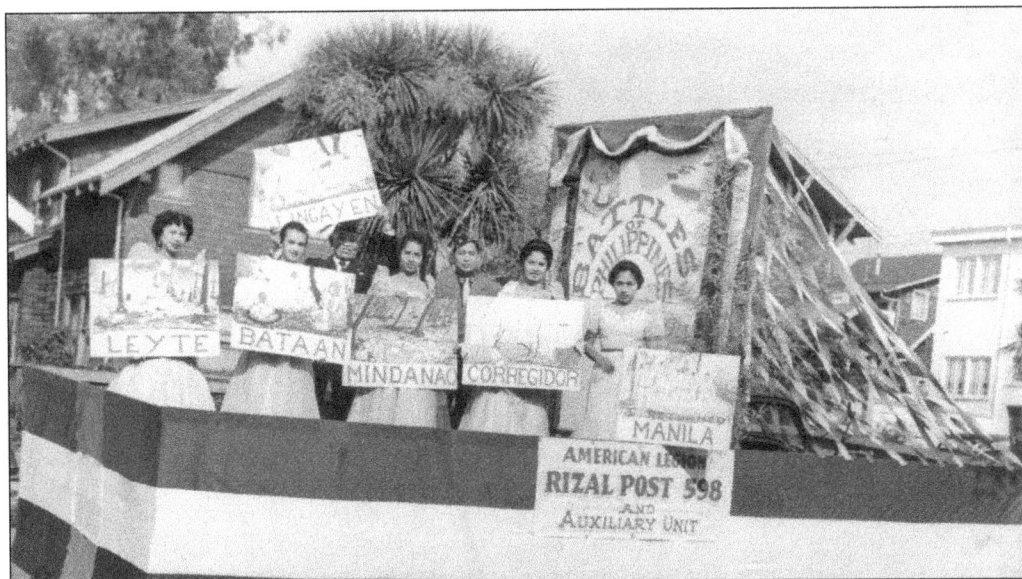

The American Legion Rizal Post 598 Auxiliary Unit, whose members were wives of the veterans, participated in many events with the post. This float, entered in a c. 1950s Veteran's Day Parade, shows the places where battles took place in the Philippines during World War II. (Photograph by Alex Hipol; courtesy of Dennis Ubungen.)

The Catmon township organization celebrated many of their town fiestas in Alvarado's ISDES Hall. The events highlighted Filipino culture through folk dancing, folk songs, and a night of music and dancing for all the celebrants. Performing a traditional Filipino dance are unidentified, Dan Branzuela, Isabel Loyola, unidentified, Cleope and George Montecillo, Filomena Gurrea, and Tommy Branzuela. (Photograph by Alex Hipol.)

Ernie Tanuatco and his band played for many of the Filipino dances and parties in the early 1940s and 1950s at Jenny Lind Hall in Oakland. Their music consisted of songs from the swing era, as well as cha-cha. The group was popular with the "bobby-sock" and jitterbugging crowd as well as with elegant ballroom dancers. (Above, courtesy of Vangie Buell; below, courtesy of Terry Acebo Davis.)

Marie Mendoza Rivera Yip sang "La Paloma" in her sister Lenora's home on Ninth Avenue in Oakland after Sunday dinners, which included chicken adobo, pancit, and pinakbet with lots of steamed rice. Marie was accompanied by her uncle Eddie Rosario, on flute, and other Manong (elders) friends. In *Seven Card Stud with Seven Manangs Wild*, Marie wrote about her mother's cleaners in Oakland Chinatown in the 1940s. (Courtesy of Marie Mendoza Rivera Yip.)

Flory Bautista, an accomplished singer in the Philippines, put her natural talent to use at community events after her arrival in 1947. In this photograph, she sings the popular World War II song "I'll Be Seeing You." The venue was Jenny Lind Hall, a favorite site for dances, weddings, baptisms, and holiday celebrations. Flory also sang in the Filipino choirs at St. Mary's and St. Anthony's Catholic Churches. (Courtesy of Teresita Bautista.)

These city kids, Anthony, Joseph "Joey," Michael, and Fatima, take a break to enjoy country life. Their father, Guillermo Valerio, a *pensionado*, studied at San Jose Teachers College and aspired to be a mathematician. Their mother, Presentacion, was a schoolteacher in the Philippines. Guillermo worked as a cook, waiter, and math tutor for the University of California, Berkeley football team. Their family belonged to St. Anthony's parish in Oakland. (Courtesy of Joseph Valerio.)

Many of the Filipino men working as farm laborers were able to house their families on the farms where they worked. Celedonio Rabello worked and lived on the Bailey ranch in Mission San Jose. His children, Teddie, Rosita, Martin, and Boyd, are shown from left to right in this 1950s photograph next to newly plowed land with the beautiful San Jose Hills in the background. (Courtesy Rosita Rabello Valerio.)

As more of the Manongs (elder men) brought their families to the United States, the Filipino community began to expand. This fact is documented in this 1957 photograph of cousins in the Tabisaura, Caranay, and Narito families taken on Bay Farm Island after the arrival of the Narito family to the United States. (Courtesy of Ponciana Caranay.)

Relatives drove miles to spend time with one another. This c. 1951 photograph includes Josephine and Carlos Pastrana from Seaside (near Monterey), who were visiting their cousins Carole and Arlinda Caranay, who lived on Bay Farm Island in Alameda. Bay Farm provided a lot of play space for kids as well as ample space to hold family parties. (Courtesy of Ponciana Caranay.)

Daniel Begonia was a communications expert with direct contact to General MacArthur during World War II. After the war, Daniel and his family worked and lived on the Amling-Devore Nursery in Livermore, known for beautiful roses. Daniel's wife, Consuelo Tecson, also worked at the nursery, and in the summer, their son, Danilo, worked with them. Danilo Begonia is a professor at San Francisco State University in Asian American studies. (Courtesy of Danilo Begonia.)

Bay Farm Island in Alameda had many truck farms that hired Filipinos as their main laborers. These truck farms supplied seasonal vegetables to the Oakland stores. The farm laborers were called "vegetable gardeners" because they worked with vegetables. From left to right in this c. 1950 photograph, Honorio Hipol, Mateo Caranay, and Isidro Dumo are bunching radishes on the Ratto farm around 1950. (Courtesy of Engracia Hipol.)

In the 1950s, many families who lived on Bay Farm Island moved into nearby cities when their farmhouses were condemned. Families continued to gather on weekends for celebrations. Eleanor Hipol and Arlinda Caranay celebrated their birthdays at the Hipols' Oakland home on Fourth Avenue and East Eighth Street near Peralta Park (across from the Oakland Auditorium), which had a merry-go-round and train ride. (Photograph by Alex Hipol.)

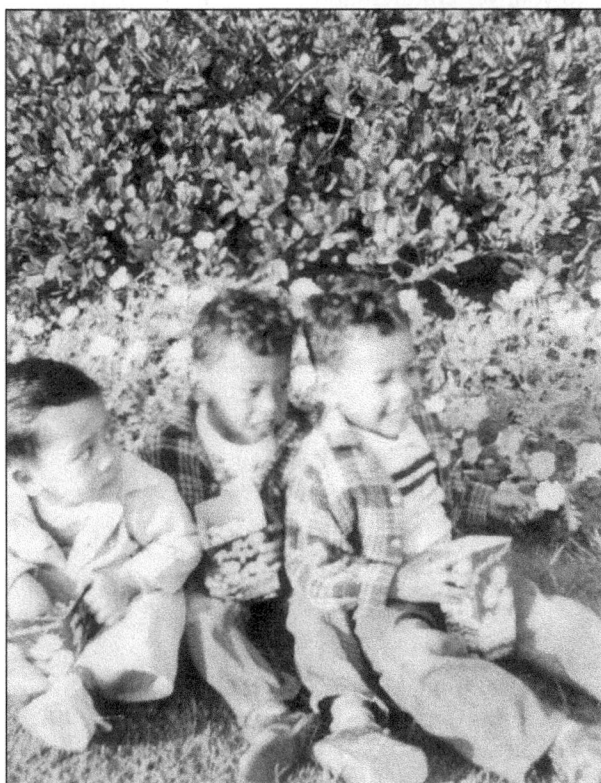

Domingo Hipol, Frank Sarmiento Jr., and Raymond Sarmiento (left to right) were photographed at Lake Merritt in Oakland. The Sarmiento boys' father, Frank Sarmiento Sr., immigrated in the 1920s. Frank Sr., his wife, Margaret, his daughter, Francis, and his two sons lived on Bay Farm Island in the late 1940s. An entrepreneur, his businesses included fish sales and delivery in Oakland and a grocery store and restaurant in Delano. (Courtesy of Engracia Hipol.)

49

Joe Marzan and his family were longtime residents of Alameda. As with many Alameda Catholic families, Joe and his wife brought their children up as members of St. Philip Neri Catholic Church parish on High Street. Here they celebrate the sacrament of Holy Communion for the two oldest children, Delerie and John, with their two younger children and other Marzan relatives and friends. (Photograph by Alex Hipol.)

In the 1950s, many of the Manongs returned to the Philippines to take a bride. Manual Saltivan, who was one of the 11 Saltivan brothers and cousins to come to the United States in the 1920s, was married to Marciana in 1955. This photograph depicts their wedding celebration in the United States with other Saltivan relatives. (Courtesy of Saltivan family.)

David Savellano celebrated his birthday around the 1960s at their home in the Fruitvale district of Oakland. The Savellano family were members of the American Legion Rizal Post 598 and active in St. Anthony's Catholic Church parish, where their children attended grammar school. David is now an architect and an artist. (Photograph by Alex Hipol.)

Isidro Luluquisen (seated second from right) cut sugarcane in Hawaii from 1929 to 1942. After World War II, he married Marcela Ramello and moved to Oakland to work at the Oakland Army Supply Center, then Ryerson Steel in Emeryville. In 1959, Marcela and daughter Esminia immigrated, and one year later, Evelyn was born. Evelyn's first birthday celebration (at Tenth and Castro Streets near Swans and Housewives Markets) was a reunion of family, friends, and town-mates. (Courtesy of Evelyn Luluquisen.)

Canuto Lorono Aranaydo worked on the Nakashima Nursery located at 1195 145th Avenue in San Leandro from 1957 to 1966. About four families and several single men lived and worked at the nursery. Each family, including Aranaydo's, was given housing while employed but did not fraternize with the owners. Families became close, adopting *ninongs* and *ninangs* (godfathers and godmothers, respectively). The proud father, Canuto, is shown with (from left to right) Linda, Michael, Bobby-Joe, and Sonny. (All courtesy of Sonny Aranaydo.)

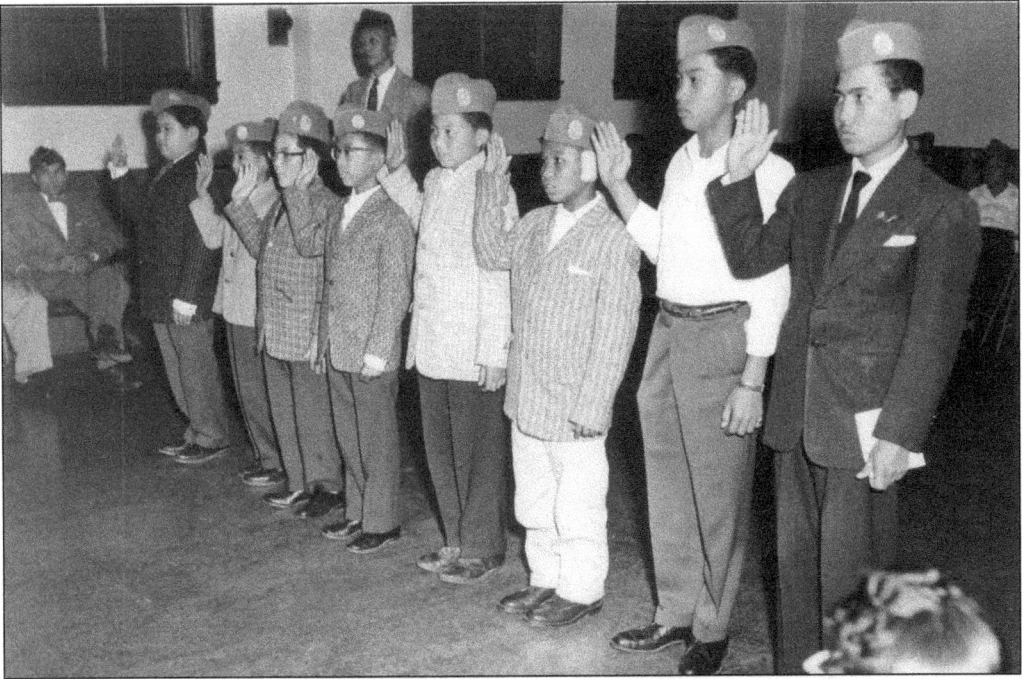

The American Legion Rizal Post 598 established a unit for the Sons of the American Legion. This picture, taken around 1958, shows the Sons taking their membership oath. Pictured are, from left to right, Alex Valerio, Danny Taay, Domingo Hipol, Eddie Pabros, Robert Taay, Tedirenio Hipol, Avelino Laigo, and Hector Hipol. (Courtesy of Domingo Hipol.)

Andy Asercion and Barbara Angel's wedding brought their families closer. From left to right are Anita Angel, Andy Asersion, Barbara Asercion, Cecilia Angel (maid of honor), and Dianna Angel. All dresses were made by Andy's mother, Paz Asercion, famous for her designs and skill in creating traditional Philippine fashions and contemporary styles. People came from afar to have their Filipino formal wear custom made by her. (Courtesy of Cecilia Angel.)

Primitivo Sonido Sr. immigrated in 1919 as a *pensionado* to study agriculture. He graduated from UC Berkeley in 1937 but did not return to the Philippines until he was stationed there during World War II. There he met his wife, Erudita Cabaltea. Erudita came as a war bride in 1949, and they had six children. Primitivo retired after working for 25 years at the Naval Air Station in Alameda. (Courtesy of JoeAnne Tuazon.)

Amado Tuazon Sr. brought his family to the United States in 1962 where they lived in Oakland. He was the first of his brothers to come to the United States. In 1964, he moved his family to Alameda. His wife, Modesta, worked in retail at the South Shore Center and in downtown Oakland. (Courtesy of Danny Tuazon.)

54

Celebrations, similar to town fiestas, were held at the home of Honorio Hipol in Oakland. There was always the roasting of a pig over an open pit in the backyard. Manongs would be on hand to rotate the pig until it was cooked. The men would dominate the kitchen, preparing the Filipino dishes (pancit, lumpia, pinakbet, chop suey) and striped bass or smelt caught in Alameda or purchased in Chinatown. (Courtesy of Engracia Hipol.)

Eustaquio "Oliver" Valerio was a member of the first squadron of the Filipino Aviators Club in 1939. He served in the U.S. military during World War II and was stationed in the Philippines where he met Carmen. Oliver and Carmen got married on April 8, 1945. Their children's names are Alex, Cesar, Virgil, Carmenata, Benjamin, Mary, Monica, Raymond, Melissa, Dennis, Rosalie, and John. (Courtesy of the Valerio family.)

Jimmy Vittero owned two fishing boats, *Lucky Day 1* and *2*, and docked them at the Berkeley marina. From left to right, Jimmy Vittero, C. Bustillos (who owned the Sportsman Cannery), and their volunteer deck-hand, Tom Ellioff, regularly motored out onto the San Francisco Bay and beyond to catch their limit of albacore, salmon, and whatever was in season. Vittero's daughter, Blanch Brown, is a professional dancer and dance instructor. (Courtesy of Tom Ellioff.)

The skipper of the "Lucky Day #1", C. Bustillos, owner of the "Sportsman Cannery", Berkeley and friend Tom Elioof went albacore fishing and brought them back for canning and smoking.

Ben Mendoza grew up in North Oakland where no other Filipino families lived in the 1940s. As a young girl, his mother, Angela, worked as a live-in housekeeper for two spinster sisters. The sisters gave her an allowance and saved the balance of her salary for a down payment on her house in North Oakland when she got married. They purchased the house for her and then transferred ownership when Filipinos were allowed to own property in the 1950s. (Courtesy of Elizabeth Mendoza Megino.)

Benny + the 36 lb.

Times Star Sports

Saturday, November 26, 1977

PAGE 13

Alamedan caught fish bigger than himself
165-pound fish landed off Treasure Island
Angelo Casabar fights sturgeon for almost hour

An Alameda man caught a fish bigger than himself—but he isn't satisfied—yet.

It isn't the biggest sturgeon ever caught in San Francisco Bay, but if Angelo Casabar keeps trying—and he intends to—chances are he will land it.

Fishing off Treasure Island, Casabar, 68-year-old retired cook, landed a sturgeon weighing 165 pounds and measuring more than 70 inches.

After an hour struggle, and using 25 pound test line, Angelo was able to get the huge fish into his 14-foot outboard boat along with himself and an excited poodle dog.

"Skipper", the dog, who wears a red jacket and is a constant companion of his master, had one of his most exciting days trying to help get the big sturgeon aboard.

The fish, the man and the dog filled the little boat as Angelo headed to the Central Bait Shop, 641 Central avenue, to recount the experience, which is once in a lifetime, but Casabar was scanning the waves off the shores of Alameda today wondering if any bigger sturgeon were there awaiting to be caught.

In August of 1975, Angelo hooked a sturgeon, weighing 88 pounds.

But the most recent catch, weighing 165 pounds, is heavier than Angelo at about 155, and is taller, unofficially at 70 inches, than Casabar at 5-6.

Casabar, who resides with his wife at 1502 Pacific Avenue, has finished the San Francisco Bay and Delta region waters every chance he could since 1929.

He was employed for years by the late "Cy"" Williams of Alameda at two of his restaurants—the Steak Dock and the Alameo—before his retirement several years ago.

Bill Stone, owner of the Central Bait Shop, who keeps track of such things says Casabar's is the biggest reported there in the past 20 years. The second largest weighed 100 pounds.

In 1977, Angelo Casabar, a fisherman at heart since 1929, caught a 165-pound, 70-inch sturgeon off Treasure Island. This was the second time he was noted for making a grand catch. Angelo immigrated to the United States in 1927 and during the war worked on a transport ship that brought supplies to the troupes in the Philippines. (Courtesy of Engracia Hipol.)

Felipe Estaban loved to go fishing in the San Francisco Bay and delta regions. This was quite a catch! (Courtesy of Esteban family.)

Keeping Filipino culture alive,
Mrs. Serrano taught folk dances
to children and teens. These two
photographs were taken at the
"Balintawak Review" in 1954. In
the top photograph, Mrs. Serrano's
daughter, Corazon, danced
with her partner. In the bottom
photograph, the Cariniosa dance
is being performed by, from left
to right, Dick Aquino, Juanita
Savella, Bonifacio Santos, and
Linda Mangiben. (Both courtesy of
Linda Mangiben Japzon.)

Filipino Mothers of America presented "Balintawak Review" at the Oakland Auditorium (now the Henry J. Kaiser Convention Center). The "Balintawak Review" presented a night of cultural dances and a fashion show of traditional Filipino fashion. Dancers in the bottom photograph are, from left to right, Ann Galvan, Durlyn Mangiben, Gloria Galvan, and Linda Mangiben. (Both courtesy of Linda Mangiben Japzon.)

After he worked at Mare Island in Vallejo, Baldomero D. Tecson opened the Elite Pool Parlor located on Ninth near Franklin Street in Oakland. The business opened in 1941 and was a local meeting and gathering place for Filipinos and their friends through the 1960s. Besides being a place to shoot pool, musicians played through the evening to entertain the customers. At left is Tecson, the proprietor of the Elite Pool Parlor; the bottom photograph shows some of the customers standing outside the establishment. Cigars and cigarettes were also sold in the pool parlor. (Left, courtesy of Dottie Ross from Bohol Circle Inc., 1949, Souvenir book; below, courtesy of Lorraine Nicholas Rollins.)

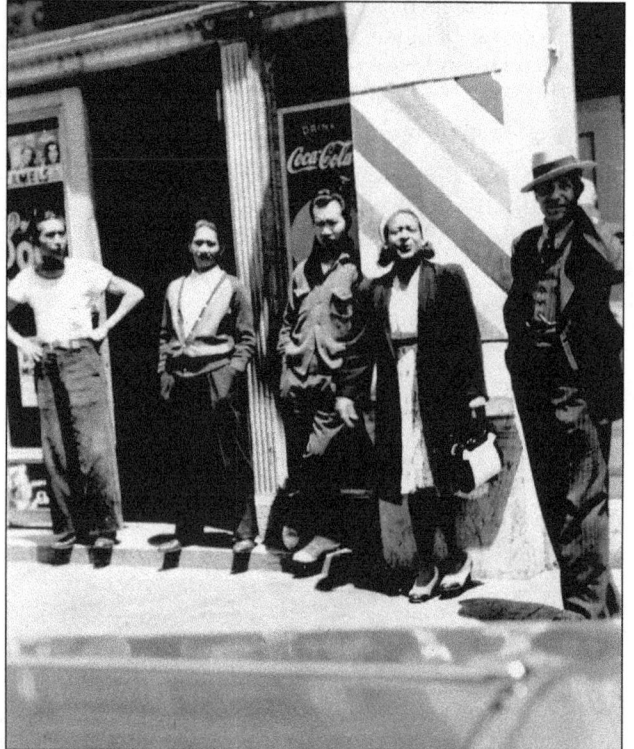

Many Filipinos became insurance agents with various companies. Max A. Villamor was a district agent of the Central Life Insurance Company of Illinois, who had a local office in Oakland. This is a copy of his advertisement placed in the Bohol Circle Souvenir Book of 1949. (Courtesy of Dottie Ross.)

Life Insurance is something that young men can best afford but Old Men most appreciate.

"Call or Write Me for Personal and Confidential Service"

Individual Life • Children's College Fund Salary Saving • Mortgage Protector • Retirement Income Partnership Group • Health and Accident Hospitalization

★

MAX A. VILLAMOR, District Agent
CENTRAL LIFE INSURANCE COMPANY
OF ILLINOIS

Marvin Building	515 Oak Street
24 California Street	Oakland, California
San Francisco, California	Higate 4-0280
SUtter 1-6342 Room 507	

Maria Mendoza Rivera purchased a dry cleaning business at 816 Franklin Street from a Japanese American family who were sent to an internment camp during World War II. The Philippine Cleaners and Laundry Agency was one of the Filipino-owned and -operated businesses in Oakland Chinatown in the 1940s. Standing outside of the cleaners is Frank Saltivan. (Courtesy of Eva Saltivan.)

61

Pedro A. Lauron came to Oakland from the Philippines in 1920 via Hawaii with his wife, Mei. From 1950 to 1957, he was the owner of a grocery store located at 601 Twenty-second Street in Oakland. This photograph includes, from left to right, ? Pantano, Mei Lauron, Pedro Lauron, Rose Pantano (a relative visiting from Louisiana), and an unidentified neighborhood child. (Courtesy of Gloria Samson.)

Marcelline "Siling" Nicholas owned the California Market, complete with meat, liquor, produce, and canned goods, on Sacramento Street near Ashby Avenue from 1941 to 1960. One daughter, Emily, worked full-time in the store; her son, Wesley, cut meat at night; and another daughter, Lorraine, stocked shelves at night. The store was once picketed by Grocery Union until they learned it was a family-owned and -operated business. (Courtesy of Lorraine Nicholas Rollins.)

Parts of Oakland Chinatown were known as "Filipino Town" to the Filipino community. Here many Filipino-owned businesses flourished from 1940 through 1960. The Elite Café, located on Franklin Street at Ninth Street, was a favorite to the Filipinos. The café changed hands over the years but continued to be heavily supported by Filipinos. (Courtesy of Dennis Ubungen.)

Family and friends pose in front of the Elite Café on Franklin Street at Ninth Street in Oakland. The Montecillo family was enterprising, owning several businesses in Oakland Chinatown. From left to right are Aling Tibon, Linda Montecillo, Eliang Montecillo, Marilyn Tecson, Nenen Tibon, unidentified, Lagring Tibon, Joe ?, Tommy Branzuela, and Pedro Montecillo. (Courtesy of Linda Montecillo.)

Franklin Electrical Shop was located on Ninth at Franklin Street, two doors down from the Elite Café. The proprietors were Cleope and George Montecillo. (Courtesy of Linda Montecillo.)

The Manila Café, owned by Cleope Montecillo and Eliang Montecillo, was located in Oakland Chinatown. This Filipino-owned business thrived from the 1950s through the 1960s. (Photograph by Alex Hipol.)

List of Filipino Owned Businesses Located in Oakland's Chinatown from 1940 -1960

1	Kalapati Lodge #515, Legionarios Del Trabajo (LDT) (1945)	815 Franklin
2	Philippine Cleaners (Marie Rivera, owner) (1942-1947)	816 Franklin
3	Jose Domingo's Barber Shop (1943)	825 Franklin
4	Domingo's Barber Shop (Domingo Gapuz, owner) (1948)	825 Franklin
5	Elite Café (1954-60's)	903 Franklin
6	Filipino Community Church (1940)	920 Franklin
7	Filipino Methodist Church (1943)	920 Franklin
8	Cortez Barber Shop (1960)	638 Webster
9	Cortez Pool Hall (1943)	718 Webster
10	Dan's Barber Shop (1960)	810 Webster
11	Philippine Federation of American, Inc (1930)	1007 Broadway
12	Central Life Insurance Company of Illinois (Max A. Villamor, District Agent)	515 Oak
13	Matt's Barber Shop (Matt O. Tinoga, owner)	406 7th
14	Restaurant (Gerardo and Leonarda La Rosa, owners) (1949)	419 1/2 7th
15	Barber Shop (M. Macagba, owner) (1943)	366 8th
16	La Union Barber Shop (1948)	366 8th
17	Sergie's Barber Shop (1954)	366 8th
18	Photography Studio (Cipriano Tibon, owner)	378 8th
19	Barber Shop (George Catambay, owner) (1940-90's)	404 8th
20	Barber Shop (S.L.Cortez, owner) (1948)	411 8th
21	Barber Shop (Ponce Barrios, owner) (1943)	460 8th
22	New Radio Shop (George & Cleope Montecillo, owners) (1943)	9th & Franklin
23	Elite Pool Parlor (Baldomero Tecson, owner) (1941-1960's)	412 9th
24	Manila Café / Pool Hall, 1961 (Cleope Montecillo, owner)	11th & Webster
25	Western Life Insurance Co. (Augustine C. Lopez, Agent)(1949)	577 14th
26	Manila Café / Pool Hall (Cleope and Eliang Montecillo, owners)	928 Franklin

Pictured here is a historical map of Filipino-owned businesses in Oakland Chinatown from 1940 to 1960. (Courtesy of Ellie Hipol Luis.)

At the age of 25, Ambrose Loyola became interested in boxing. He trained under Max Bear in Oakland. Recognized as a good competitor, he was signed on as a featherweight boxer and became known as "Speedy" Loyola. His boxing matches were held at the Oakland Auditorium in 1933. Ambrose Loyola owned a service station on Levee Street (now Union City Boulevard) in Alvarado (now part of Union City). His business thrived until Highway 17 was constructed. To help the family finances at that time, his second daughter, Lulu, willingly took a one-year leave from college to work full-time. In the 1970s, Isabel Loyola opened a childcare center, on Smith Street near Alvarado Road. This area is designated "Old Alvarado," an historic area of Union City. A commercial building was erected in 2001 on the site of the childcare center dedicated to the Loyola family legacy. In the Loyola building are Toppings Too and Paddy's Coffee House, popular community gathering places serving delicious food and beverages. (Both courtesy of Lulu Tipping.)

From the 1940s to 1960s, the Claremont Hotel, where many Filipinos worked, was a place for high-society events. Standing in front of the hotel from left to right are employees Victoriano Soto, two unidentified, Raymond Marzan, Mariano Abuan, and Gerardo Nimendez. By the time of Mariano Abuan's retirement, he had worked his way from busboy to event planner/supervisor. (Courtesy Madeline Abuan.)

George Catambay's Movieland Barbershop was the last Filipino Town business to close in Oakland in the mid-1990s. He was among the many barbers who had shops in Oakland. Old-timers recalled barbers Anacito Fernandez, Johnny de Guzman, Sergie Fernandez, and George Torio. George Catambay's son, George Jr., at one point also styled hair in the shop before becoming a dentist. (Courtesy of Mel Orpilla.)

Queen contests were associated with township organizations as well as with the American Legion Rizal Post 598. Most of these contests were based on popularity in which the candidates had to sell tickets for votes. The title of queen went to the contestant who sold the highest number of tickets. The court consisted of a queen, princesses, flower girls, and all their escorts. (Courtesy of Arlinda Caranay Fujii.)

Caroline Caranay, Miss Freedom, was one of the princesses in the 1966 Miss American Legion Rizal Post 598 contest. Caroline's escort is Domingo Hipol. The annual New Year's Eve event, held at the Oakland Veterans Building across from Lake Merritt, was later changed to Mrs. American Legion, and Caroline's mother, Ponciana Caranay, was the first reigning queen. (Courtesy of Arlinda Caranay Fujii.)

Three

CHANGING
DEMOGRAPHICS

"Project Manong" in the early 1970s was to renovate a two-story hotel on Sixteenth Street in downtown Oakland. Volunteer students from the University of California, Berkeley formed the Pilipino Youth Development Council (PYDC) and worked with the elderly Filipino men (Manongs). Project Manong created an opportunity for the youth to learn from the manongs about their life challenges as the first Filipino immigrants to the United States. Inspired by that experience, some of those youth moved forward in their careers to become educators and social justice activists. (Courtesy of Filipinos for Affirmative Action [FAA] archives.)

69

Filipino students joined student movements to establish ethnic studies academic programs, defend affirmative action programs, and oppose the Vietnam War. Filipinos participated in and led marches like this one through UC Berkeley's iconic Sather Gate around 1969. The Tagalog banner on the left translates to "Don't Be Meek," encouraging fellow students to break from their silence to express their political voice. (Courtesy of FAA archives.)

President Marcos's 1972 declaration of martial law in the Philippines was a controversial issue. Prominent in the national anti-martial law movement was the *Katipunan ng mga Demokratikong Pilipino* (KDP), based in Oakland. The staff of the KDP newspaper *Ang Katipunan* is pictured here clockwise from the top right: Rene Cruz, Nene Ojeda, Emil de Guzman, Vince Reyes, Wicks Geaga, Eddie Escultura, Nancy Rocamora, and Christine Araneta. (Courtesy of Vince Reyes Jr.)

In the 1970s, a changed concept of "self" emerged. Vietnam veterans like Ben Luis (with Ellie Hipol Luis) came home from the war to a social climate that demanded change, promoted individual freedom, and included a sense of "just let me be myself" attitude. Electronic rock music was on every radio channel, and avant-garde was hip. Fashion reflected the young people's changing philosophy on life. (Photograph by Edgar Valdehueza.)

Lydia Gorrez (left) immigrated to the United States in 1970 to pursue a doctorate in education. She became a special education teacher at Lockwood School in Oakland. She is pictured here with members of the multicultural program committee for Oakland schools. Her children subsequently joined her and settled in the East Bay and on the peninsula. (Courtesy of Christine Araneta.)

The Campaign Against the Marcos Dictatorship (CAMD), pictured here at a 1984 conference in Berkeley, played a major role in educating the U.S. public and Congress about the Marcos dictatorship in the Philippines. The CAMD was part of the "left wing" of the broad opposition to martial law. Two years later, the People's Power movement in the Philippines would succeed in overthrowing the dictator. (Courtesy of Vince Reyes Jr.)

Evelyn Pragasa immigrated to the United States in 1978 to join her husband, who was in the U.S. Navy. She found work with the City of Oakland where she helped build a Filipino employee group that hosts an annual celebration of June 12 (Philippine Independence Day). From left to right are Eric Pragasa, Dina Abellera, Sheryll Pragasa, Connie Sabo, Rom Pragasa, Caroline Rosaroso, Evelyn Pragasa, and Grace Pragasa. (Courtesy of Evelyn Pragasa.)

Pilipino Youth Development Council (PYDC) in the late 1970s was sponsored by the Filipino Immigrant Services, a direct services agency. They ran a summer job training and education program funded by the CETA (Comprehensive Employment Training Act) program. PYDC sponsored activities that bridged the language and cultural gap between immigrant and U.S.-born Filipino youth. (Courtesy of FAA archives.)

Pete Masilang (left), Cery Rosal, and Dominador Maranon (far right) are at the Filipino Senior Citizens Center in Oakland. The senior center was the site of many Filipino community activities in the mid-1980s, not only for seniors but for the whole community. The senior center was a meeting place for those who immigrated before World War II and those of the post-1965 wave of immigrants. (Courtesy of FAA archives.)

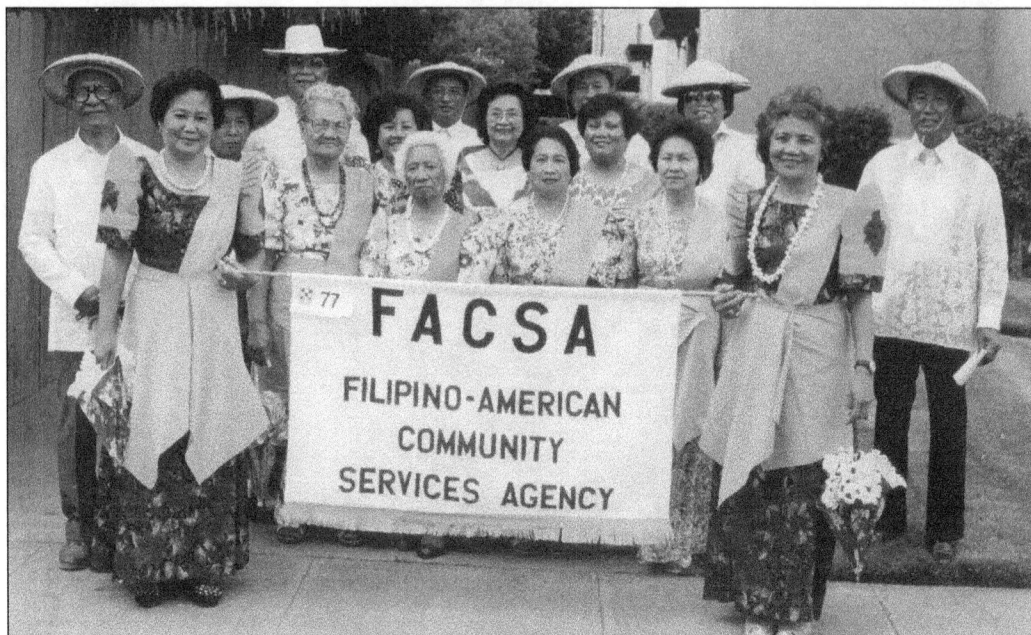

Filipino American Community Services Agency (FACSA) in Alameda is a community service organization founded in 1992. Their goal is to improve the quality of life of the persons it serves, regardless of race, color, sex, age, and benefits. FACSA started the Midway Homeless Shelter in Alameda, which is still in operation. (Courtesy of Liberata Canalin.)

The East Bay Women's Group was founded by Charito Benipayo in 1998 with 22 charter members. This social services organization has a broad scope of areas to which they cater. Members pictured here are, from left to right, Marcie Gatutan, Elena Bongon, Isolina Cadle, Cynthia Gaabucayam, Charito Benipayo, Nora Clautero, Leonore Montes, and Cora Ariosa. (Courtesy of Isolina Cadle.)

In 1967, the Love brothers opened a restaurant in Oakland Chinatown at Ninth and Webster Streets, which then moved to Eighth Avenue and East Eighth Street until 1987. Love's Pagan Den was at the forefront in presenting Filipino food in a formal dining setting in Oakland. From left to right are Frank Megino, Ben Love, unidentified, and Art Love. They now own the bed-and-breakfast Ginger Island in Hilo, Hawaii. (Courtesy of Elizabeth Mendoza Megino.)

In 1988, Evelyn Tuazon opened the Leamington Florist at 365 Nineteenth Street in Oakland. The business has been successful for almost 20 years. At one time, she also owned the adjoining restaurant. In this photograph, Lyn sells flowers to a customer. Lyn and her husband, Dan, have four children and currently live in Alameda. (Courtesy of Evelyn Tuazon.)

Lamberto and Consolacion Batongbacal immigrated to the United States in 1978 with six of their nine children. The last two children arrived in 1980. The oldest settled in Australia. Their children now hold positions of significant responsibility for employers such as the City and County of San Francisco, San Diego County, Microsoft, AT&T, Fremont Bank, and State Compensation Insurance Fund. To date, the senior Batongbacals have 11 grandchildren. (Courtesy of Edwin Batongbacal.)

After a five-year separation, Eduardo Valladares (with camera) was reunited with his family at the San Francisco airport on February 18, 1994. Ed received a religious worker visa in 1988 and has worked at Filipinos for Affirmative Action since 1989, helping newcomers navigate their new country and become citizens. Pictured from left to right are Bernhardt, Eduardo Jr., Teilhardt, Dorothy, Ed, Walter, and Ed's wife, Esther. (Courtesy of Ed Valladares.)

Alfredo (a chemist) and Norma (a pediatrician) Paragas have built a successful medical practice in Fremont since 1983. Dr. Norma Paragas's father gained citizenship fighting alongside the Americans in the Philippines during World War II. In 1974, she came to the United States. She is one of the few pediatricians with her own practice in Fremont. (Courtesy of Ligaya Paragas.)

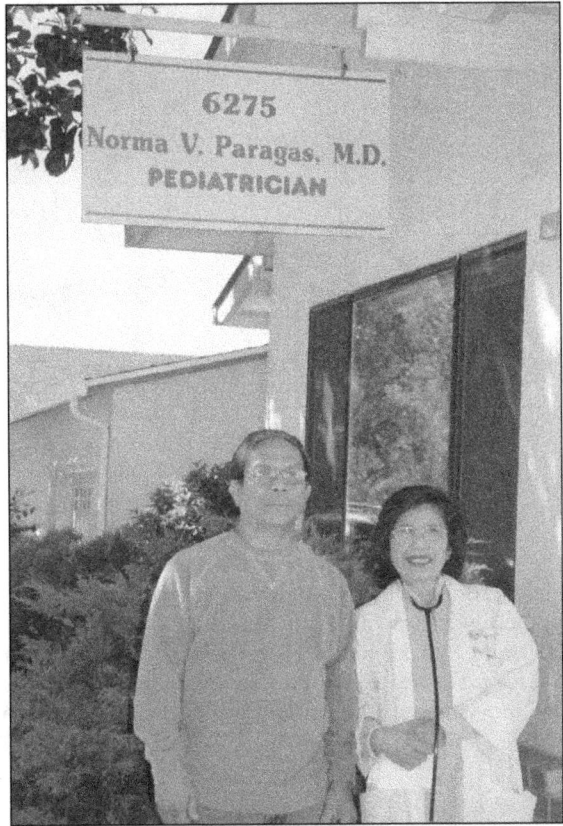

Filipino medical professionals who settled in the San Francisco Bay Area maintain their ties to the Philippines. Participants in an annual medical mission to the Philippines pose before leaving. From left to right are J. Querubim, retired military; Mila Enriquez, nurse; Dr. Lilia Ferrer Ibabao, anesthesiologist; Emily Ibabao Marley, nurse; Dr. Tino Ibabao, surgeon (and primary mission organizer); Luchi Labos-Simpao, teacher; and Fatima and Rey Cocquia. (Courtesy of Luchi Labos-Simpao.)

Helen Toribio was an Asian American studies professor at City College of San Francisco and San Francisco State University. She coauthored *The Forbidden Book: The Philippine-American War in Political Cartoons*, edited *Seven Card Stud with Seven Manangs Wild*, and contributed to *Legacy to Liberation* and Asian American studies publications. Helen was an activist in the anti-martial law movement and in immigrant and civil rights issues. (Courtesy of Teresita Bautista.)

Catherine Ceniza Choy is an associate professor of ethnic studies at University of California, Berkeley. Born and raised in New York City, she earned a Ph.D. in history from University of California, Los Angeles in 1998. She is the author of *Empire Care: Nursing Migration of Filipino American History*. Her husband, Gregg Choy, is a lecturer in ethnic studies at University of California, Berkeley. (Courtesy of Yuji Yasue.)

Maria Luisa Penaranda, an artist, teacher, and writer, received her master's in education from California State University, East Bay. Maria Luisa teaches Tagalog at Stanford University, CSU East Bay, and Ohlone College. She coordinated the Filipino American Art Exposition in San Francisco in 1990. She is a member of the Philippine American Writers and Artists and has exhibited her paintings in Bay Area art galleries. (Courtesy of Oscar Penaranda.)

Proudly standing with mother, Isabel, Mia Luluquisen earned her doctorate in public health from UC Berkeley and received the Henrik Blum Award for Distinguished Social Action for cofounding Oakland's San Antonio Neighborhood Health Center and co-establishing Hawaii's Sariling Gawa Youth Council. Mia currently manages evaluation, health education/training, and strategic planning for the Alameda County Public Health Department and teaches at San Francisco State University's Community Health Education/Masters in Public Health program. (Courtesy of Isabel Luluquisen.)

Cora Tellez is founder, president, and CEO of Sterling HSA, a leader in tax-advantaged health care benefits called health savings accounts. She serves on the boards of First Consulting Group (NYSE: FCGI) and Crescent Healthcare and on the advisory board of PracticeFusion and several nonprofit organizations, including the Cowell Foundation, Philippine International Aid, Institute for Medical Quality, and Mills College. (Courtesy of Cora Tellez.)

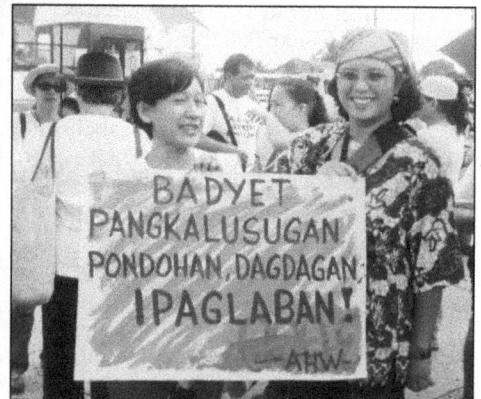

Veronica Isip Macapagal (Adams), left, was born in San Fernando, Pampanga, and immigrated in 1969. She is a counselor faculty at CaPS on staff at Eden Counseling, working with families, kids, and teens. Mylene Amoguis Cahambing (right) grew up in Marikina, Metro Manila, and immigrated in 1981. She currently works as a public health nurse in a local county; the photograph shows a public health "exposure" with the Health Alliance for Democracy (HEAD) while in the Philippines. (Left, courtesy of Veronica Macapagal; right, courtesy of Mylene Cahambing.)

Cecilia Angel was in the navy WAVES for three years (1958–1961), stationed at the Oak Knoll Naval Hospital in Oakland. She was one of the first six women to be trained in intensive care in California. She resides with her mother, Marina, now 88 years old, in Manteca. (Courtesy Cecelia Angel.)

Rene de Guzman is a senior art curator at the Oakland Museum of California and is responsible for developing projects and building collections. Former director of visual arts at the San Francisco Yerba Buena Center for the Arts, Rene obtained his bachelor's degree in art practice from UC Berkeley and taught in the graduate fine arts program of the San Francisco Arts Institute and the California College of Arts. (Courtesy of Rene de Guzman.)

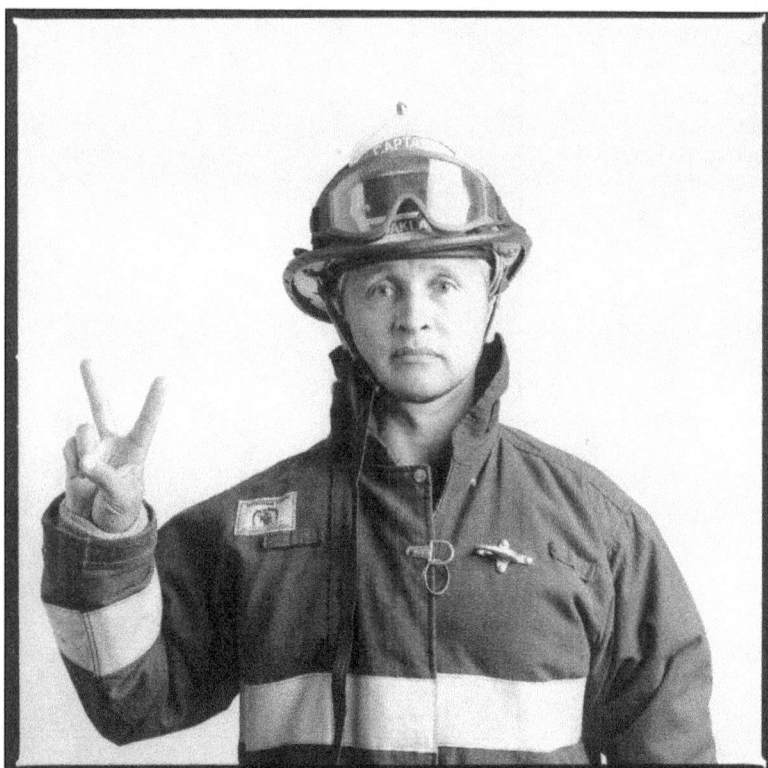

Oakland fire captain Ray Gatchalian was the off-duty firefighter who organized brave residents of the Broadway Terrace neighborhood to stop the raging Oakland Hills inferno in 1991. He was also an entrepreneur, philanthropist, farm worker advocate, and Vietnam War veteran. In 1980, he produced *In No One's Shadow*, a documentary on Filipinos in the United States. He was a champion for peace his whole life. (Courtesy of Gatchalian family.)

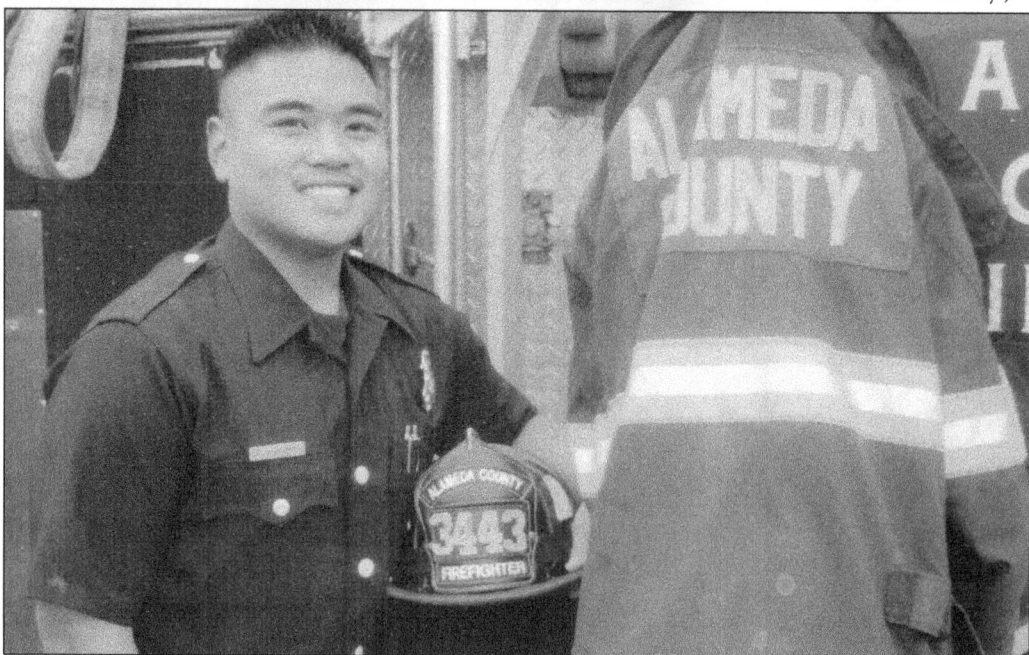

Ryan Garcia is a proud member of the Alameda County Fire Department (ACFD). He grew up in Alameda and is a 1998 graduate of Encinal High School. Before being hired, he served as a volunteer to the ACFD as a reserve firefighter and worked as a seasonal firefighter with CAL-FIRE. (Courtesy of Ryan Garcia.)

In 1977, after air force duty, John Mangiben (left) was hired as a police technician for the City of Alameda. In 1979, he was hired as the first Filipino police officer in the Alameda Police Department, and in 2002, he retired. Tyman Eugene Small (right) is the great-grandson of buffalo soldier George Knox. Tyman studied law before becoming an Oakland police officer in 2006. (Left, courtesy of John Mangiben; right, courtesy of Lorraine Nicholas Rollins.)

Stacey Vilas was a police officer for 25 years with the Oakland and Madison Police Departments. She created educational videos on pedestrian, traffic, and driving safety for youth, volunteered to promote traffic safety for the community, and organized tennis programs for underprivileged children. Standing with her is former deputy chief of police John Ream, who was born and raised in the Philippines. (Courtesy of Evangeline Buell.)

Roberto Mercado Tal was born in the Philippines and came to the United States in the mid-1950s. He is a graduate of the University of California San Francisco's School of Dentistry and has had his own practice for 14 years. This photograph was taken during a client consultation session at the Native American Health Clinic in Oakland where he has also worked for the past 17 years. (Courtesy of Robert Tal.)

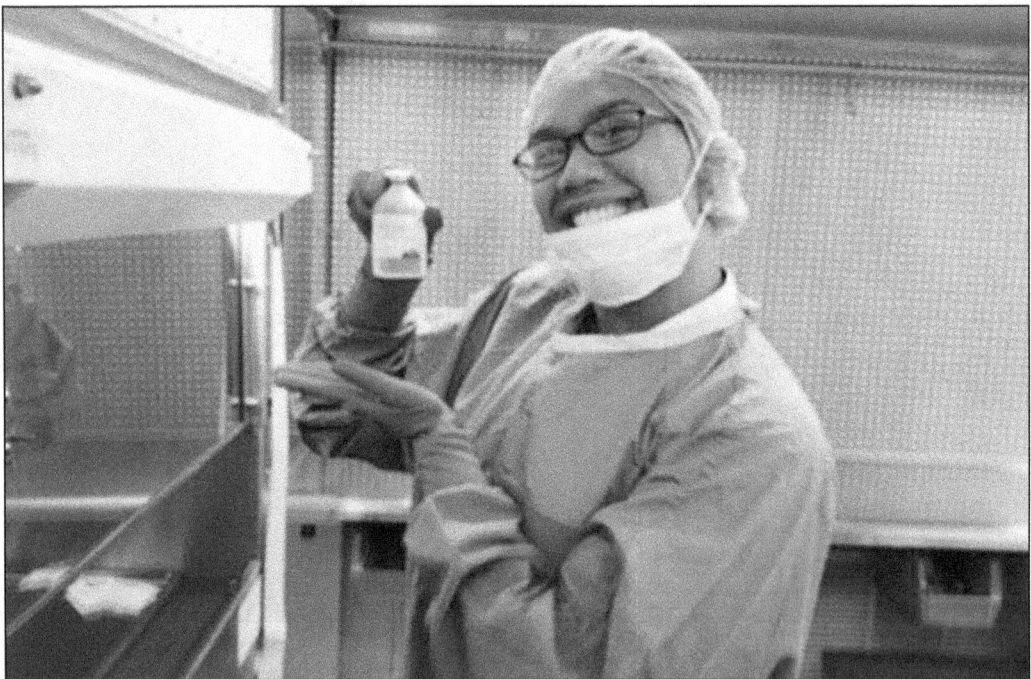

Ruby Pontemayor was hired at St. Joseph's Hospital in Stockton as a clinical pharmacist after graduating in 2005 from the University of the Pacific. Ruby grew up in Guam, Japan, and the East Bay before pursuing her goal to become a pharmacist. (Courtesy of Ruby Pontemayor.)

Dr. Jorge Emmanuel trained in chemistry, engineering, environmental management, and public health. He is a consultant to the World Health Organization and other international agencies and governments and is a founder of the Filipino American Coalition for Environmental Solidarity. He is one of the authors of *The Forbidden Book: The Philippine-American War in Political Cartoons.* (Courtesy of Jorge Emannuel.)

Faustino "Tito" M. Cruz, SM (Society of Mary), is executive vice president and academic dean of the Franciscan School of Theology in Berkeley. He has a doctorate in theology and education from Boston College and is an ordained Roman Catholic priest. He has ministered with migrants and refugees and worked as a consultant, educator, community organizer, and pastor in the United States, Latin America, and the Philippines. (Courtesy of Vangie Buell.)

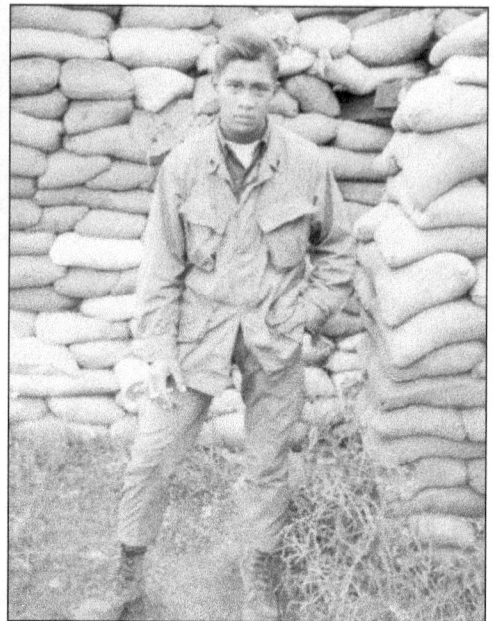

Paul Nonan (left) and Ernesto Marlan (right) enlisted in the military after high school. Both served in Vietnam in the late 1960s. With the draft in effect, enlistees could choose their branch of military, an option not available to draftees. Ernie served in the U.S. Marines and is photographed in a bunker on the front lines of DaNang, where fighting was heavy. (Courtesy of Ellie Luis and Ernie Marlan.)

Allyson Tintiangco-Cubales, as a member of the Pilipino American Alliance at UC Berkeley in 1992, marched alongside students of MECHA (Movimiento Estúdentil Chicano de Atlan) to commemorate the grape boycott. Allyson is now an associate professor of Asian American studies at San Francisco State University. (Photograph by Edgar N. DeVera; courtesy of Allyson Tintiangco-Cubales.)

Affirmative action opened doors in the construction trades. Megio Galicia (second from the right), operating engineer, was among the growing number of Filipinos who entered apprenticeship programs and built careers as construction workers. He was the driver of an earth mover until his retirement in 2006. He was also a business agent for his union for three years. (Courtesy of Teresita Bautista.)

Ben Luis completed the sprinkler fitter apprentice program and was "turned out" in the work field in 1978. He was member of Local 483, Sprinkler Fitters Union, and has been retired from the trade since 2004. He worked with Filipinos for Affirmative Action and the Ella Hill Hutch Community Center in a pre-apprenticeship training program, assisting eligible people to get into the construction trades. (Courtesy of FAA archives.)

Abba Ramos was a union organizer for the International Longshore Warehouse Union from the time he was a young hotel worker in Hawaii to his retirement in the late 1990s. His parents were sugarcane workers in Hawaii during the 1930s and 1940s, a system he likens to apartheid where workers were hostage to mill owners. He lived and organized in the East Bay for decades. (Courtesy of David Bacon.)

Legendary labor organizers Pete Velasco, Philip Vera Cruz, and Larry Itliong started the great grape strike of 1965 that inspired the creation of the United Farm Workers (UFW). In the 1970s, Pete was the East Bay organizer of the grape boycott. Pete is pictured here (third from the left) with his wife, Dolores, and friends at an Oakland memorial for Philip Vera Cruz in 1994. (Courtesy of FAA archives.)

Tessie Paredes (with her husband, Jim) settled in Contra Costa County in the 1970s where the Filipino community is now the largest Asian population. They raised two daughters and a son in Concord. Tessie was an appointee to the Human Relations Commission for many years and often spoke out on behalf of the disenfranchised. Here she supports nursing home workers during a union organizing campaign. (Courtesy of FAA archives.)

Following the tragic attacks on September 11, 2001, airport screeners were accused of a breach of security. As a result, screener jobs were federalized and nearly 30,000 airport screeners nationwide were fired. In the San Francisco Bay Area, nearly 60 percent of screeners were Filipino, and they waged a yearlong effort to preserve their jobs. Kawal Ulanday speaks in support of the screeners at a rally in Oakland. (Courtesy of FAA archives.)

The Filipino community in Union City, which represented 20 percent of the population in 2007, has elected Filipinos to public office since the late 1980s. Manny Fernandez (left) has served on the city council for six terms since 1987, the longest serving member in Union City's history. Jim Navarro (right) was elected to the school board for four years before being elected to the city council in 2005. (Courtesy of FAA archives.)

The national struggle for bilingual education was played out in Oakland through a lawsuit against the Oakland Public Schools by immigrant parents and their allies. Carlito Cardona (second from left), leader of the parent plaintiffs, was joined by teacher Cassie Lopez (left), unidentified, and Remy Reyes (right) at an Oakland School Board meeting. Plaintiffs won a settlement forcing implementation of a bilingual education plan in the district. (Courtesy of FAA archives.)

Mae Cendaña was elected a board member of Ambrose Recreation and Park District in Bay Point, Contra Costa County. Her goals are to expand recreation services for sport programs, teens, and seniors; promote the completion of the 149-acre Bay Point Waterfront Park and Trail; and continue to address safety in parks and on trails. (Courtesy of Mae Cendana.)

Tony Daysog was the first Filipino to serve on the Alameda City Council and was reelected to serve two terms until 2006, when he reached term limits. He also served as the city's vice mayor in 1998–2000 and 2002–2004. He is a master's graduate from UC Berkeley in urban planning and has an extensive background in this field. (Courtesy of Ellie Hipol Luis.)

Mario R. Ramil retired as associate justice of the Hawaii Supreme Court. He was raised in Livermore, graduated from Hastings College of Law, and was deputy attorney general in Hawaii's Ninth Circuit Court of Appeals. Pictured is the Hawaii Supreme Court in 2002: from left to right, Associate Justice Mario R. Ramil, Associate Justice Steven H. Levinson, Chief Justice Ronald T. Y. Moon, Associate Justice Paula A. Nakayama, and Associate Justice Simeon R. Acoba. (Courtesy of Gloria Omania.)

Gloria Omania (left), with daughter Joy, demonstrates courage, vision, and commitment for the betterment of the Filipino American community through social, educational, economic, and political empowerment. Inspired by her father's determination to know his civil rights and her family's *kabayan* spirit to help other immigrant families while growing up in Livermore, Gloria has built a 26-year career as chief of staff and chief advisor for California senator Tom Torlakson. (Courtesy of Gloria Omania.)

Tessie Zaragosa was aide to U.S. congressman Ronald Dellums from 1983 to 1998. She was responsible for constituent casework and represented the congressman at community events. Tessie organized the first Artistic Discovery for High School Students event for the Ninth Congressional District, which exists today. Tessie was involved in the anti-martial law movement and remains active on women's issues. From left to right are Tessie, Ronald Dellums, and Tessie's husband, Rich Carter. (Courtesy of Tessie Zaragosa.)

Immigrants and non-immigrants became active in the electoral process in the 1970s. Pictured are members of Filipinos for Riles after having hosted an Oakland mayoral candidate's forum. From left to right are unidentified, Rudy Fernandez, candidate Wilson Riles Jr., two unidentified, and Pete Masilang (on the right behind an unidentified woman). (Courtesy of FAA archives.)

Ermena Vinluan of Alameda, director-producer for the film *Tea & Justice*, won Best Domestic Documentary and Outstanding Contribution to Filmmaking at the fifth annual Queens International Film Festival (QIFF) in New York City. Longtime civil rights activist, Ermena is a script consultant, stage producer, artistic director, and lead playwright involved with FilCRA (Filipino Civil Rights Advocates) and NaFFAA (National Federation of Filipino American Associations). She is also resident artist at Julia de Burgos Cultural Center. (Photograph by Rick Cook; courtesy of Ermena Vinluan.)

Janet Stickmon—teacher, writer, and spoken word artist—authored *Crushing Soft Rubies: A Memoir*, in which she confronts her early struggle with being biracial. She says, "I learned not to see myself as half and half, but that I was 100 percent of both." Janet holds a master's in religion and society from the Graduate Theological Union and a master's in ethnic studies from San Francisco State University. (Courtesy of Janet Stickmon.)

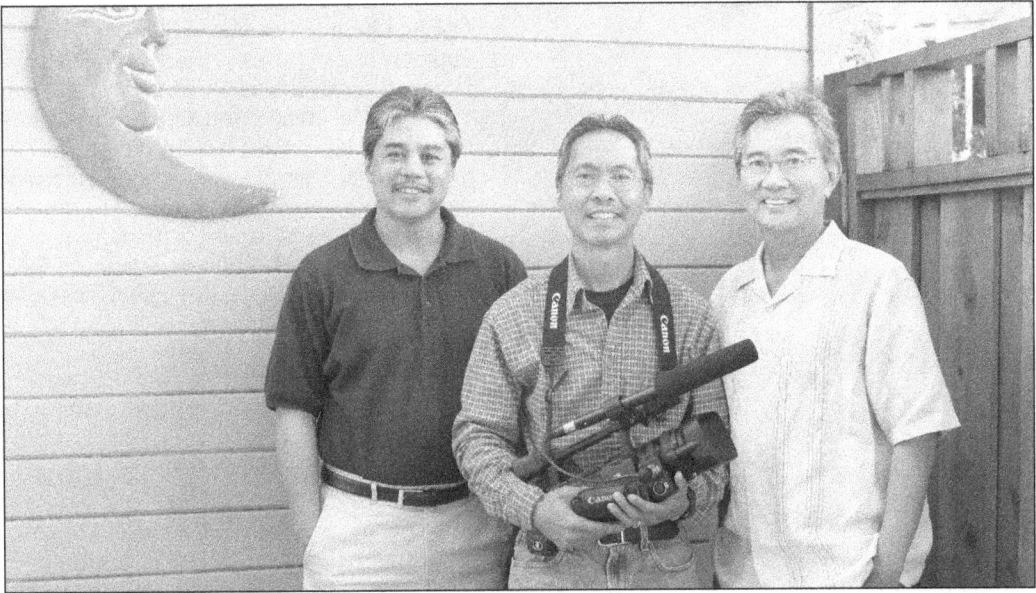

Benny Evangelista (left) is cousin to Gary (center) and Vince Reyes. Benny is a senior editor for the *San Francisco Chronicle* and produces *Pinoy Podcast*. Gary is an award-winning photojournalist, including two Pulitzer Prizes. One was for coverage of the 1989 Loma Prieta earthquake and the other for team coverage of Hurricane Katrina. Vince is special assistant to the director in Alameda County's Social Services Agency. (Courtesy of Gary Reyes.)

Producer/director Marissa Trinidad Arroy has now produced two films for PBS station KVIE. She has also worked behind the camera, directed films, and as an associate producer won the Nancy Dickerson Whitehead Award for journalism. She has a bachelor's degree from Boston College and a master's from UC Berkeley. She teaches digital filmmaking at Berkeley City College. (Courtesy Marissa Arroy.)

Daniel Giray is a teacher, choreographer, and performer in ballet, musical theater, jazz, and children's dance therapy. Daniel is the creator and artistic director of Kulintang Dance Theater. He was mentored by Danongan Kalanduyan, was a member of Palibuniyan and the Mindinao Kulintang Ensemble, and is perhaps better known to children on television for *Danny G's Incredible Learning Fun Times.* (Courtesy of Daniel Giray.)

In 2005, Ambrosio Q. Angel, also known as Skip, and his sisters created AQA Designs, a business geared to profile their individual talents as designers. Art and Exhibitions, Inc., is featuring Skip's designs in its tour of Egyptian antiquities entitled "Tutankhamen and the Golden Age of the Pharaohs." Skip's designs are not only Egyptian; he creates beaded jewelry to suit any true collector of jewelry accessories. (Courtesy of Skip Angel.)

Terry Acebo Davis was the first American Pilipina to show artwork in Samsung Hall at San Francisco's Asian Art Museum in 2004. Terry stands with her auntie, Lilia A. Acebo, before her installation *Tabing Rising*. This artwork, rising 20 feet into the rotunda and extending 30 feet into the hall, visually tells the story of her family's immigration to Oakland, California, in 1945 from war-torn Manila. (Courtesy of Terry Acebo Davis.)

Paulo Luis worked as a graphic designer before graduation from high school. He earned his bachelor of science in design and industry at San Francisco State University. He is a freehand artist and is currently working on a comic series. He is the illustrator of *Full Deck (Jokers Playing)* by Oscar Penaranda. (Courtesy Paulo Luis.)

Contributing authors to the anthology *Seven Card Stud with Seven Manangs Wild* gathered to celebrate the second printing of the book in 2002. The Filipino American National Historical Society of the East Bay sponsored the anthology, which was edited by Helen Toribio and coedited by Evangeline Canonizado Buell, Terry Bautista, and Elizabeth Megino. A sequel to the book is in progress in 2008. (Courtesy of Vangie Buell.)

The Forbidden Book: The Philippine-American War in Political Cartoons was coauthored by Abe Ignacio, Jorge Emmanuel, Enrique De La Cruz, and Helen Toribio and illustrated by artist Carl Angel. The seminal work, which includes Abe Ignacio's collection of obscure and out-of-print cartoons gathered over a period of 20 years, received the 2005 Gustavus Myers Outstanding Book Award. (Courtesy of Carl Angel.)

Tallulah David cohosts *Speak Out* with J. C. Gonzales on ABS-CBN International. The program airs discussions on Filipino social issues such as first generation versus second, Young Fil-Ams, affirmative action, the 'Guest Worker' Program, and interracial dating. At the University of California, Berkeley, Tallulah served as the youth mentorship co-coordinator for the Berkeley Pilipino Academic Student Services, extending mentorship programs to Pilipino youth around the Bay Area. (Courtesy of Tallulah David.)

The FOB Show, a multi-performance production capturing the Filipino immigrant experience with cast members from all over the Bay Area, was presented at Logan High School in 2007. *The FOB Show*, created by Bindlestiff Studio and based in San Francisco, is the only permanent Filipino-American performing arts space in the nation presenting hundreds of events and productions annually, including theater, dance, music, comedy, spoken word, and film. (Courtesy of Mike Ricca.)

Joseph "Flip" Nunez left us too soon. He shared his life with his daughter, Dana, and grandson, Kianowa. A musician extraordinaire, Flip could play any music form and did just that with a number of famous musicians of the R&B, Latin rock/jazz, blues, and jazz genres. He has composed and arranged numerous compositions that are yet to be recorded on his behalf. (Photograph by David Bacon.)

"Lasa ng Jazz" was the first Filipino jazz concert in the East Bay. It was held at Alice Arts Center in Oakland on October 22, 1994, to benefit Filipinos for Affirmative Action. The historic lineup included Flip Nunez, Rudy Tenio, Josie Canion, Jodie Ente, Melicio Magdaluyo, and the Ben Luis Ensemble of Ted Strong, Nito Medina, and Ben Luis. Jon Jang and Jodie Ente emceed. (Courtesy of Ellie Luis.)

Since the 1970s, Evelie Delfino Sales Posch and Deo Arellano, cofounders of Mahal, have been bringing a blissful, boundless electric energy through their music to cross-cultural and multi-spiritual audiences. Transformative, timeless, sacred, divine, and earthy, Mahal sings songs of world peace, justice, and truth in many languages: English, Sanskrit, Spanish, Portuguese, Native American, German, and Filipino. Mahal's music is heartfelt and sweet yet strong, bringing one to a futuristic past or cosmic present. (Courtesy of Mahal.)

Evangeline ("Vangie") Canonizado Buell, accomplished and award-winning writer, author, activist, and musician, has performed as a folk singer/guitarist since 1952. She was recently selected as one of the 100 Most Influential Filipina Women in the United States by Filipino Women's Network and received the 2007 Global Filipino Literary Award for her book, *Twenty-Five Chickens and a Pig for a Bride: Growing Up in a Filipino Immigrant Family*. (Courtesy of Vangie Buell.)

Carlos Zialcita is known in music venues for playing his harmonica where the blues are center stage. He is also a jazz vocalist. Carlos teaches computer courses at Encinal High School, where he is the faculty sponsor for the Pilipino American Culture Club. This photograph was taken for the exhibit Filipino Musicians Through the Generations, displayed at the Manilatown Center in San Francisco. (Photograph by Angelica Cabande.)

Sugar Pie De Santo (Umpeylia Marsema Balinton) is known as a great blues singer, first-class soul singer, commanding jazz stylist, arranger, and composer. She has recorded with famous artists, and her compositions have been recorded by other artists. She has been honored on many occasions. In 2007, she received a National Rhythm and Blues Foundation award for being an R&B pioneer. (Courtesy of Samuel Martin Ribitch and Jim Moore.)

Dennis Calloway belonged to the Grammy Award–winning Zydeco band Queen Ida in the 1980s and continues to play with the local East Bay band Motordude Zydeco. Zydeco is indigenous to southwest Louisiana. He works for CalTrans as a landscape architect. (Courtesy of Dennis Calloway.)

Ben Luis was attracted to music in the early 1950s when he heard his mother, Lumy Competente, sing on the radio in Stockton. He shares his musical talent teaching youth, helping them move their musical talents to their fullest potential. He supports community events and activist movements with his music and has recently been honored by Chi Rho Omicron (San Francisco State University) for paving the way for future musicians. (Courtesy of Ben Luis.)

The Kalayaan band formed in 1973 and played at local venues, including the Pauley Ballroom at University of California, Berkeley. They had a funky R&B music base that drew a large following. From left to right are (first row) David Yamasaki, Richard Aquon, and John Del Rosario; (second row) Julian Melendres, Chris Corpuz, Ross Wilson, Dean Boysen, Jesse Manibusan, and Kenny Penalver. (Courtesy of Kenny Penalver.)

Combining rock, pop, and blues, MotherHumbuckers produces a unique sound. They have backgrounds from kali martial arts to theater to music video. They play originals and cover tunes, have been reviewed in the *San Francisco Chronicle*, and appeared on The Filipino Channel's talk show *Speak Out*. Pictured from left to right are Martin Reyes, Jose Marco, Ollie Pabonan, and Rocky Reyes. (Courtesy of Rocky Reyes.)

The musicians in Little Brown Brother have been playing professionally since the 1970s. Each of them brings flavors and spices from a variety of music genres—Latin, jazz, R&B, blues, classical, rock, and swing—"on our terms." Pictured from left to right are Chris Planas, Mio Flores, Carlos Zialcita, Mike Fernando, and Ben Luis. (Courtesy of Carlos Zialcita.)

Ted Hipol cut his first vinyl at the age of six, and in the 1960s, he formed the band D'Illusions as the pianist and lead vocalist. He graduated from San Francisco State University (with a bachelor's in music, voice emphasis) and continues to sing with various groups hired for private corporate parties. He is also an independent contractor who works on local homes and small businesses. (Courtesy of Ellie Luis.)

Rick Quisol plays guitar, ukulele, kazoo, and drums and is a lead vocalist. He is a member of the Frisky Frolics (Tin Pan Alley Troubadours), which was voted Best Band for the New Depression by *Bay Guardian's Best of the Bay 2001* and SF Weekly Wammie Nominees. They were featured in the George Lucas documentary *Profligate Genius* and *Tin Pan Alley: Soundtrack of America*. (Courtesy of Rick Quisol.)

Students from James Logan High School in Union City established themselves as a vocal group (APEX), gaining popularity in the Filipino community. Several years later (*c.* 1997), with personnel changes the group became known as KAI. They were televised on the *Bruce Latimer Show*, KQED, the Sports Channel, and KTSF. Pictured from left to right are Anthony-Chris Lorenzo, Leo Chan, Errol Viray, Andrew Gapuz, and Andrey Silva. (Courtesy of Ben Luis.)

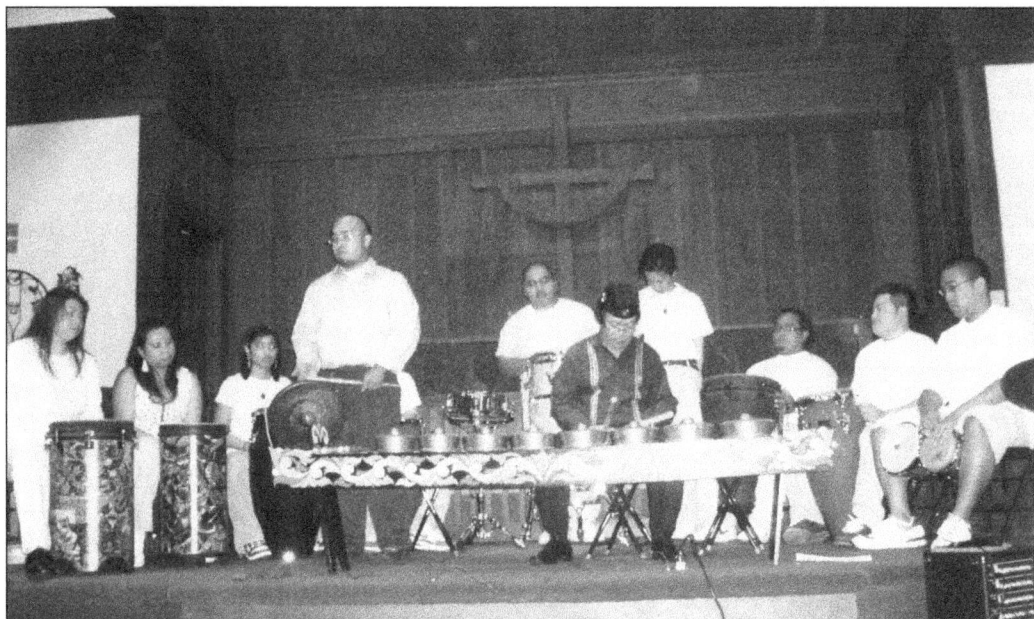

Joachim Luis (standing, left) seriously began his vocal career as a voice major at San Francisco State University. He has conducted choirs for cultural events, performed in operas, and sang with the Oakland Bay Area Community Chorus. He studied Kulintang with Master Danongan Kalanduyan as a core member of the Ating Tao Drummers. Currently he is pursuing a master's degree in voice performance at Roosevelt University in Chicago. (Courtesy of Joachim Luis.)

Raised in Alaska, Titania Buchholdt grew up with indigenous Native Alaskan music and dance and learned traditional beadwork, ryegrass basket making, and skin sewing. After graduating from UC Berkeley and Georgetown Law School, she studied Kulintang music and traditional dance with award-winning teacher Master Danongan Kalanduyan and other master artists. She has performed at hundreds of venues and is preparing two books on Kulintang music. (Courtesy of Titania Buchholdt.)

Kaloy Kaymanggi (left) is a DJ and program producer at KPFA Radio in Berkeley. He hosted a radio show called *Pilipino Ourstory* for Pilipino History Month in 2006, presenting Pilipinos and their art forms. Amado Tuazon (right) and Dance-a-way Productions have been providing music for various events since 1983. The production expanded to video services and big-screen rentals. (Courtesy of Kaloy Kayamanggi and Amado Tuazon.)

Golda Supernova proclaims that she writes and sings for the "loud at heart." Hailing from Oakland by way of Alaska and Manila, Golda performs unique rock songs with the intention of lifting the whole room a little closer to outer space. (Courtesy of Golda Supernova.)

Oakland-based poet/playwright, performer, and educator Aimee Suzara aims to provoke dialogue and build community through poetry, movement, and theater. Her writing, including the play *Pagbabalik (Return)* and the chapbook *the space between* (Finishing Line Press), explores themes of home, homeland, migration, and the body. Recognizing her role on the continuum of queer, Filipino, women of color, and activist and literary histories, Suzara inspires current and future generations to tell their own stories. (Photograph by D. Samuel Marsh.)

Manila-born Barbara Jane Reyes was raised in Fremont. She completed her undergraduate degree in ethnic studies at UC Berkeley and a graduate degree in creative writing at San Francisco State University. She has published two books, *Gravities of Center* and *Poeta en San Francisco*, and is the recipient of the prestigious James Laughlin Award of the Academic of American Poets. (Photograph by Edwin Leynes; courtesy of B. J. Reyes.)

From left to right are Mary Bonzo, Lewis Suzuki, Trudy Bonzo, and Gloria Bucol. Mary and Trudy are the daughters of Jerry and Blanch Bonzo, who met as students at the University of Nebraska. Blanch was Dutch-Irish-Welsh American, and Jerry had come from the Philippines to study. Lewis Suzuki is a prolific social activist painter. Gloria Bucol grew up in Merced and moved to Fremont, where she was a school administrator. (Courtesy of Trudy Chastain and Evelyn Luluquisen.)

Members of the Philippine Ethnic Arts and Cultural Exchange (PEACE) traveled to the Philippines in 1996 to learn about the issues of the indigenous peoples of the Cordillera region. Pictured are (first row) Mel Orpilla, Ben Nobida, and DonnaLynn Rubiano; (second row) Abe Ignacio, the mayor of Sagada, Anita Escandor, Bill Sorro, and Joe Arriola. (Courtesy of Anita Escandor.)

James Sobredo (left) is a filmmaker and published academic in ethnic studies. Al Robles (center) is a poet, activist, and community leader who was at the forefront of Asian American literature and community issues, most notably in the fight against eviction of elderly residents and demolition of the International Hotel in San Francisco. Ben Mendoza (right) worked as a chemist and is published in *Seven Card Stud with Seven Manangs Wild*. (Courtesy of James Sobredo.)

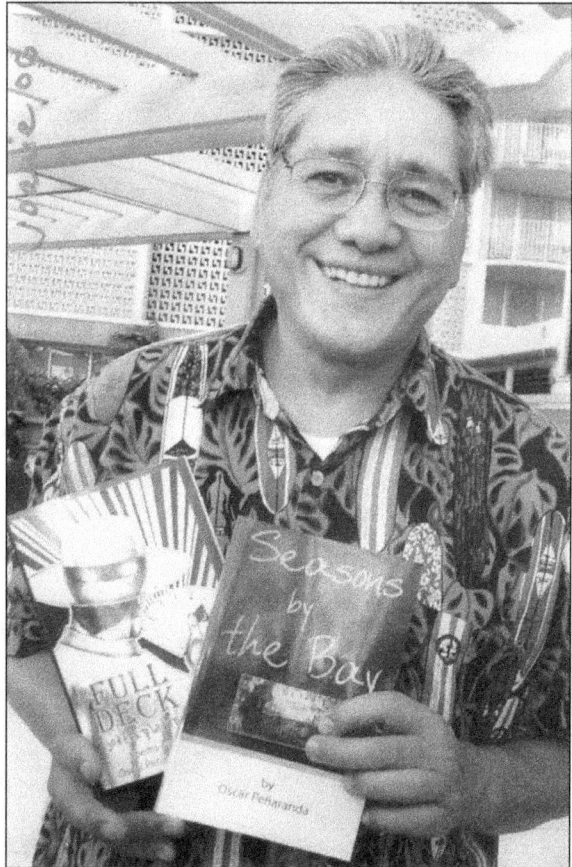

A community activist, educator, storyteller, poet, and martial artist, Oscar Penaranda is an established and important California writer. He was at the forefront of Filipino, Philippine American, Asian American, and third world literature. He teaches Filipino American history and Tagalog at Logan High School in Union City. (Courtesy of Oscar Penaranda.)

In 1990, the Bohol Circle Thunderstars won first place in the Annual Delano Pilipino State Basketball Championship. Basketball is a favorite sport that brings the Filipinos together. The Bohol Circle—founded in 1936 in Oakland, now in Alameda—espouses honesty, thrift, modesty, and perseverance. Shown are, from left to right, (kneeling) Phil Abello, Mark Leyva, Leo Sacramento, Steve Kim, Eric Fortes, and Michi Langfeldt; (standing) Mark Mesquida, unidentified, Jim Dailey, unidentified, Noel Aquino, and Vince Encelan. (Courtesy of Mark Leyva.)

From left to right, Mateo Reyes, Godfrey Antonio, and Nathan Reyes are black belt martial arts instructors in tae kwon do. Mateo trained since he was 10 years old and is a first-degree black belt. Nathan trained since he was five years old and is a second-degree black belt. Both are third-generation Oaklanders. They plan to open their own martial arts school in the East Bay. (Courtesy of Vince Reyes Jr.)

Daniel Moreno ran track for Chabot College in Hayward in the early 1970s and now owns Sonlight Surf Shop in Pacifica. He is featured in a documentary film exploring the complexities of immigrant social and emotional experiences. *Gift of Barong* is about two generations of Bay Area Filipino American surfers who traveled to the Philippines to be immersed in the culture and surf the islands and rediscovered themselves. (Courtesy of Daniel Moreno.)

Rock climbing was a way of life for Evelyn Luluquisen from the early 1980s to the 1990s. One of few female climbers at the time, she frequented Donner Summit, Tuolumne Meadows, Yosemite Valley, and Courtright Reservoir. Evelyn decided that Cathedral Peak in Tuolumne Meadows would be her last climb after a near-death experience. Now she takes urban youth to climbing gyms and on outdoor adventures in Northern California. (Courtesy of Evelyn Luluquisen.)

Tuhan (Master) Mel Lopez teaches the Villabrille–Largusa Kali System, a Filipino martial art founded by the late Grandmaster Floro Villabrille and later systemized by Grandmaster Ben Largusa. Dating to before the Spanish invasion of the Philippines and traditionally taught only to chosen individuals, Kali is now practiced by thousands around the world, continuing this treasured art of Philippine heritage. (Courtesy of Mel Lopez.)

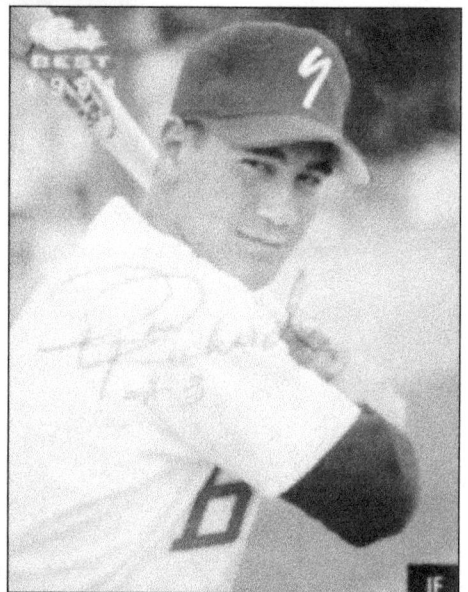

Alameda has turned out some outstanding baseball players over the years. Francis Paiso (left), a star pitcher at Encinal High School (class of 1997), was drafted by the Cleveland Indians as a pitcher. Ron Richards (right), a star player at Alameda High School in the late 1980s, was drafted to play shortstop for the Dodgers. (Left, courtesy of Francisco Paiso; right, courtesy of Ron Richards.)

Four

THE JOURNEY CONTINUES

The Filipino community in the 21st century is multigenerational and multicultural. It is deeply rooted here in the East Bay. The family of Evangeline "Vangie" Canonizado Buell represents five generations, starting with 1870 buffalo soldier Ernest Stokes (her grandfather) and his daughter, Felicia Bunag Stokes. Vangie is third-generation; daughters Danni, Nikki, and Stacey are fourth-generation; their daughters Quiana and Brielle and sons Joshua and Jamil are fifth-generation. They are mixed Irish, English, Jewish, Chinese, Spanish, African American, and Filipino. (Courtesy of Vangie Buell.)

Anthony and Liberata Canalin immigrated with five children in the mid-1950s. Soon after their arrival, three more children were born. Antonio retired after 36 years at Pacific Bell, and Liberata retired after 20 years at the Naval Air Station. This photograph, taken in the early 1990s, includes their multiracial grandchildren. A few more generations have since been born. (Courtesy of Thelma Richards.)

Vicky Santos was born in Chicago. She served as the first executive director of Filipinos for Affirmative Action, chairman of the board for Asian Community Mental Health Services, and contributed to the anthology *Seven Card Stud with Seven Manangs Wild*. In this photograph, Vicky is with her son, Thomas, and husband, Nuno Rebelo, of Portugal. (Courtesy of Vicky Santos.)

Baylan, Caroline, and Elizabeth Mendoza Megino are three generations of Filipinas. Elizabeth retired from UC Berkeley as undergraduate advisor for Asian American studies and ethnic studies. Baylan is director of Prepaid Legal Services, Inc., serves on the El Cerrito Chamber of Commerce, and is the national assistant secretary of Filipino American National Historical Society. Caroline, a student at Albany High School, is active with community youth organizations. (Courtesy Elizabeth Megino.)

Mariano Abuan arrived in the early 1920s. He owned a pool parlor and provided recent arrivals with rooms free of charge. In return, he asked boarders to leave usable items for the next boarders. In the 1970s, Mariano and his wife, Eleanor Telles, marched with others against the eviction of elderly residents from the International Hotel in San Francisco. This photograph captures five generations of their multicultural family. (Courtesy of Madeline Abuan.)

Bride Trina Villanueva, who emigrated from the Philippines in 1984, and groom Hector Preciado, who emigrated from Mexico in 1980, represent the expanding multicultural community in the East Bay. They met at the Greenlining Institute, a social justice organization in Berkeley. Together they work and socialize in a multiethnic network of immigrants and non-immigrants and are seen in this photograph with friends and family in September 2007. (Courtesy of Dwayne S. Marsh.)

Daniel and Dionisia Manaois, surrounded by family members, celebrated their 50th wedding anniversary in 1997. Daniel immigrated to the United States in 1976. Working two jobs, he was able to bring over his family of eight children over the course of 10 years. The Manaois children chose occupations such as administrator, accountant, technician, engineer, letter carrier, and naval officer. Today Daniel and Dionisia have 12 grandchildren. (Courtesy of Judith Manaois Olais.)

Edna Biscocho Murray worked overseas in Singapore for two years before immigrating to the East Bay. She has worked for Alameda County for 18 years. She is active in Community Overcoming Relationship Abuse (CORA) and a performer in both the English and Tagalog productions of *The Vagina Monologues*, sponsored by the Filipino Women's Network. Edna and her husband, Clinton, raised their son with strong family values. (Courtesy of Edna Murray.)

George Guzman immigrated in the 1920s and worked at Edy's Restaurant for 30 years to support his wife, Leonila, and daughter, Linda. Linda and her son, Dean, received their bachelor of arts degrees together from UC Berkeley. From left to right are (sitting) Leonila Guzman, Anthony, his wife Grace, and their children; (standing) Norm and Linda Haraguchi, Dean, his wife Ann, and their children. (Courtesy of Linda Haraguichi.)

Over the years, the Filipino youth have become more involved with a variety of organized sports. Josh Van Bourg has been a member of Golden Bear Gymnastics of Berkeley for nine years. His last competition, the Baleri Liukin Invitational in Texas, awarded him a medal in the floor competition. (Courtesy of Eva Saltivan Van Bourg.)

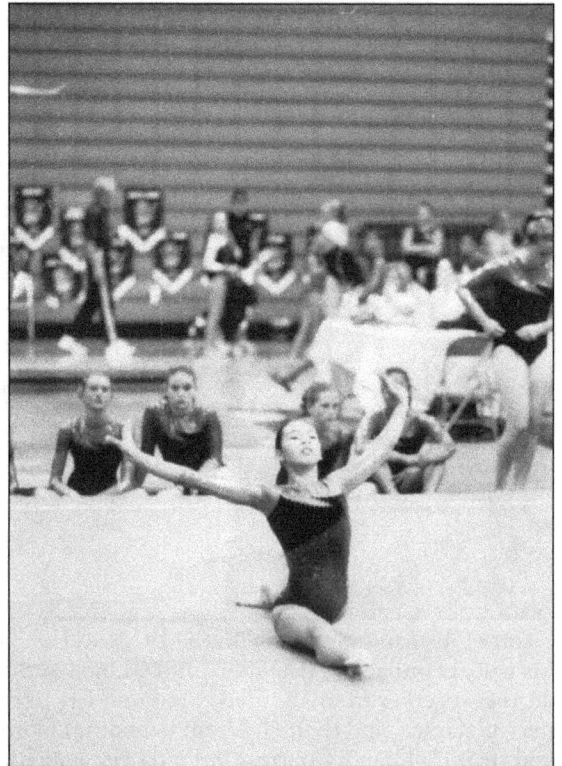

Jade Pavao (Filipino/Portuguese) was a member of Alameda Gymnastics for seven years and now performs jazz and hip-hop with Dance 10 in Alameda. (Courtesy of Janeane Pavao.)

Dan Tuazon has owned Alameda TaeKwonDo Academy since 1990. The studio serves a large number of young children in classes for various skill levels. This photograph captures one of Dan's classes of children in action. (Courtesy of Dan Tuazon.)

Andrew Nelson is third-generation Filipino. He has been with San Francisco Fencer's Club since he was 12 years old. He has competed throughout California and nationally (Dallas, New Mexico, and Arizona). He enjoys the strategy and physical elements of the sport and hopes to compete internationally. (Courtesy of Mary Nelson.)

Banyuhay (pronounced bah-nyew-hay) is an acronym for the Tagalog phrase "Bagong Anyo Ng Buhay," meaning "A New Outlook on Life." Founded in 1991, the Banyuhay Group sings traditional spiritual songs and folk songs at every Sunday mass, alternating between St. Patrick's Catholic Church in Rodeo and St. Joseph's Catholic Church in San Pablo.

Henry Nelson is third-generation Filipino. He has loved to sing with the Pacific Boychoir Academy (PBA) based in Oakland since he was seven years old. He has toured with the PBA all around the United States as well as to Brazil, France, Italy, and Denmark. He sang mass at the Vatican's St. Peter's Basilica in Rome and at Versailles in France. (Courtesy of Mary Nelson.)

Filipino American Employees Society of the City of Oakland hosts an annual Fiesta Filipiniana to celebrate June 12, Philippine Independence Day. Hundreds of city employees come out to enjoy Filipino food and folk dance performances in the sunshine. Pictured here is former Oakland mayor Jerry Brown introducing a folk dance performance to the appreciative crowd. (Courtesy of Evelyn Pragasa.)

The Holy Spirit Church in Fremont has a youth ministry that teaches confirmation classes and helps out with church functions. The youth are leaders in the Catholic community, reaching out to other teenagers. Youth ministry members organize and celebrate the youth mass and sing together in a choir. (Courtesy of Nicole Siababa.)

Above left, Filipino World War II veterans from San Pablo, with their wives, are part of a 15-year national campaign to pass the Filipino Veterans Equity Act. The veterans, now over 80 years old, fought for the United States during World War II. When the Rescission Act of 1946 was passed, their U.S. citizenship and veteran status was revoked. In 1991, U.S. citizenship was reinstated. Their veteran status has yet to be restored. At right, immigrant rights activists, locally and nationally, campaigned against the Simpson-Mazzoli Bill. Speaking against the bill in 1982 are Lillian Galedo (center), Filipinos for Affirmative Action; with activist attorneys Manny Romero (left) and Jose Padilla (right) at a press conference at the American Civil Liberties Union of Northern California office in San Francisco. They continue to advocate for immigrant rights. (Courtesy of FAA archives.)

Above left, the struggle for immigrant rights has inspired the younger generation. On May 1, 2007, in Oakland, Katie Joaquin led a rally and march demanding legalization of undocumented immigrants and an end to raids on homes and businesses. She helped mobilize nearly 8,000 immigrants and concerned activists. As an organizer for Filipinos for Affirmative Action, she also educates workers about their rights in the workplace. Stephen Funk from Hayward (far right) served in the U.S. Marine Corps and became a symbol of resistance to the war in Iraq for refusing to be deployed in 2003. Motivated by his commitment to non-violence, Stephen filed for discharge as a conscientious objector, prompting his military arrest. Next to Stephen is his sister, Caitlin, who helped organize community support for his successful release from the brig. (Courtesy of FAA archives.)

Filipinos in Union City have been active in shaping policies that benefit the city as a whole. In the mid-1980s, the New Haven Unified School District of Union City had the highest suspension and expulsion rates in the East Bay until the Concerned Parent Group won reforms that were less punitive and aimed at keeping students in school. (Courtesy of FAA archives.)

In the late 1990s, RACE (Regional Alliance for Community Empowerment)—a youth organizing project—authored, advocated for, and won the passage of Union City's first Youth Policy. It promised to increase funding for youth services and programs. (Courtesy of FAA archives.)

Bindlestiff Studio's producers of *The FOB Show* conducted workshops with Filipino students at James Logan High School to produce a skit that uniquely expressed their experience as immigrants and children of immigrants. The students developed the characters, wrote the script, and performed onstage to a full house in March 2007. (Courtesy of Mike Ricca.)

Pilipino Youth Coalition (PYC) of Union City celebrated its 12th anniversary in 2008. PYC speaks out for the rights of immigrants, for increased services for youth, against war, and against human rights abuses. PYC members participated in an immigrant rights march in San Francisco in September 2006. PYC members exemplify the self-respect and dignity that inspires Filipino youth to continue advocating for social justice. (Courtesy of Jamison Boyer.)

BIBLIOGRAPHY

Alameda Times Star.

Amerasia Journal, Asian American Studies. "New Inquiries into the Socioeconomic Status of Filipino Americans in California." UCLA Volume 13, Number 1, 1986–1987.

Bohol Circle, Inc., Souvenir Book. Oakland, CA: 1949.

Buell, Evangeline Canonizado. *Twenty-Five Chickens and a Pig for a Bride: Growing Up in a Filipino Immigrant Family.* San Francisco, CA: Tiboli Publishing, 2006.

Cabanila, Ray, and Floyd Bongolan, eds. *Legionarios Del Trabajo, Blue Book.* 3rd ed. 1975.

Filipinos for Affirmative Action photograph archives.

Hyung-chan, Kim, and Cynthia C. Mejia. *Filipinos in America, 1898–1974.* Dobbs Ferry, NY: Oceana Publications, 1976.

Ignacio, Abe, Enrique de la Cruz, Jorge Emmanuel, and Helen Toribio. *The Forbidden Book: The Philippine-American War in Political Cartoons.* San Francisco, CA: Tiboli Publishing, 2004.

Images of America series, Charleston, SC: Arcadia Publishing.

Legionarios Del Trabajo, *Blue Book. Summer '49.* Published by the Fraternal Council, Legionarios Del Trabajo in America, Inc.

Oakland City Directories: 1927, 1930, 1943, 1948, 1950, 1960.

Lott, Juanita Tamayo. *Common Destiny: Filipino American Generations.* Lanham, MD: Rowman and Littlefield, 2006.

Toribio, Helen, ed. *Seven Card Stud with Seven Manangs Wild: An Anthology of Filipino-American Writings.* San Francisco, CA: Tiboli Publishing, 2002.

Visit us at
arcadiapublishing.com

www.ingramcontent.com/pod-product-compliance
Lightning Source LLC
Chambersburg PA
CBHW080631110426
42813CB00006B/1653